# JESUS WEEPS

# JESUS WEEPS

## Global Encounters on Our Doorstep

# Harold J. Recinos

ABINGDON PRESS
Nashville

JESUS WEEPS
GLOBAL ENCOUNTERS ON OUR DOORSTEP

*Copyright © 1992 by Abingdon Press*

All rights reserved.

*This book is printed on recycled, acid-free paper.*

**Library of Congress Cataloging-in-Publication Data**

Recinos, Harold J. (Harold Joseph), 1955-
    Jesus weeps : global encounters on our doorstep / Harold Joseph Recinos.
      p.   cm.
    Includes bibliographical references.
    ISBN 0-687-03185-0 (alk. paper)
    1. Cities and towns—Religious aspects—Christianity.  2. Church and the world.  I. Title.
  BR115.C45R43   1992
253' .08968—dc20                                       92-5250
                                                            CIP

MANUFACTURED IN THE UNITED STATES OF AMERICA

TO

My daughter Claire Elizabeth Recinos

My professors in the Department of Anthropology
American University in Washington, D.C.

All persons committed to understanding human diversity as a pathway
for the construction of a more just and fraternal society.

# CONTENTS

FOREWORD . . . . . . . . . . . . . . . . . . . . . . . . . . . . . . . . . . . . . . . . 9

INTRODUCTION . . . . . . . . . . . . . . . . . . . . . . . . . . . . . . . . . . . . 15

CHAPTER ONE:   Images of the City . . . . . . . . . . . . . . . . . . . . . .21

CHAPTER TWO:   God's Sacred Place: The City . . . . . . . . . . . . . . .39

CHAPTER THREE:   The City and Globalization . . . . . . . . . . . . . . 55

CHAPTER FOUR:   Globalization: Encountering Some City Voices . .79

CHAPTER FIVE:   Pastoral Anthropology . . . . . . . . . . . . . . . . . . . 101

CHAPTER SIX:   Pastoral Anthropology and Local Immersion . . . 115

NOTES . . . . . . . . . . . . . . . . . . . . . . . . . . . . . . . . . . . . . . . . . . 133

SUGGESTED FURTHER READING . . . . . . . . . . . . . . . . . . . . . . . . . . 141

# FOREWORD

Think globally and act locally" was declared by French philosopher Jacques Ellul to be the principal challenge for the last two decades of the twentieth century. This phrase has become the theme for Earth Day and the point of entry for many interpretations of contemporary culture. "Globalization" has become an integral part of a biblically-informed vision of a more just, peaceful, and sustainable world community. A task force of the Association of Theological Schools in the United States and Canada has declared that the 1990s will be the decade of globalization. In this imaginative, poetic, and yet decidedly practical work, Harold Recinos has wedded thinking globally and acting locally. As a Latino pastor-scholar, Hal offers not only a fresh definition, but also a rich application of globalization.

For two decades I have had the privilege of being deeply involved in a series of experimental projects concerned with the globalization of theological education. The purpose of these projects is to prepare future leaders for building up a church able and willing to respond to the challenge of global witness and service. These experiments have sought effective ways to equip leaders of the church, men and women, laity and clergy, to carry on a faithful and effective ministry in an increasingly interdependent global village. For the challenge of thinking globally and acting locally to be met, participants in these projects agree that both the seminary and the church must be transformed.

The seminary must change the way it teaches; the church must adapt the way it engages in ministry. As Paulo Freire, Brazilian educator and mentor for innumerable educators in the quest for transformative education, recently declared to a group of seminary faculty, administrators, trustees, and students, "Change is difficult, but possible." In order to travel this transformational path through the kingdom of the status quo in the seminary and the church, we need experienced guides and imaginative scouts. Hal Recinos becomes both guide and scout, and in the process makes an important contribution to globalization.

Recinos' disclosures in this book await the intrepid traveler. The poetry in this volume often reveals Hal's insights in a way in which mere prose could not. Any attempt by this Anglo pastor-theologian to orient you to Hal's work would surely be a disappointment. Rather, I will share with you why I think this work is important and how it exposes some of the seductive detours that have become evident in projects in globalization, including those with which I have been involved.

First, this work provides not merely a definition of globalization, but an authentic application. One of the dangers of a preoccupation with globalization is that this effort often generates increasingly complex definitions of the meaning of globalization. In their genuine attempts to clarify the meaning of globalization, some recent projects have generated a war of words and an avalanche of academic articles. One consequence has been to divert energy from the development of experiments in globalization that might lead to the renewal of the seminary and the church. Hal, while clarifying our understanding of globalization with some fresh perspectives, constantly pushes toward application as the only legitimate test. He will settle for nothing less than the actual encounter between persons of radically different worlds. Globalization, for Recinos, focuses on the city as the sacred place where the Crucified One leads us to accompany one toward a resurrection resulting in empowerment for the fullness of life. Recinos can apply this theme both concretely and politically, because he has lived the experience himself. Hal's personal story is of being an abandoned child on the streets of the city, who passes through the crucible of drug addiction and family death to a Latino-Anglo cross-cultural encounter that by God's grace brings wholeness. Hal's powerful experience of transformation challenges each of us to be open to the "radically other" in the city for the sake of the gospel and for the renewal of the church. The mark of global conversion is local immersion. In this work the power of application is more compelling than the seduction of redefinition.

Second, this book addresses directly the specific danger for middle-class North Americans of being distracted from local engagement by an international immersion experience. There is a growing number of international educational experiences that place participants in a radically different environment and expose them to the authenticity of the struggles of Christians seeking dignity, justice, and peace for their people. For many, the authenticity of an intensive encounter with those from a radically different culture has been the catalytic factor in significant personal transformation. In a majority of cases, this transformation is marked not only by a new intentionality, but also by new behavior and a commitment for a new solidarity with the poor and marginalized who are God's favored ones. Recinos celebrates such transformations and the new alliances between North Americans and brothers and sisters in the so-called "Third World" of the global South. What Recinos highlights is the persistent pattern of immersion participants, despite their rhetoric, of neglecting, if not ignoring, the suffering and transforming potential within the cities of North America.

It is admittedly more exotic and enticing to experience this transforming encounter with the other in India or Peru or South Africa. International exchange is often "safer" since colleagues in those countries are neither as accessible to participants nor as persistent in their demands for mutuality as are brothers and sisters within our own cities. Recinos proposes that one of the primary tasks of programs of globalization is their ability to wed the global and the local.

The author addresses the reality of a globalization program so clearly because he has in fact experienced both the power and the seduction of international immersion. I had the opportunity to accompany Hal on just such a learning experience in Peru and Cuba. He acknowledged the seductive inspiration to do his anthropological research on the riches of the Peruvian religious experience, especially in the beauty of the high Andes. He found it necessary to explore and then resist this temptation in order to invest his energies in the cities of North America with special reference to the Latino community. This decision was made not primarily out of obligation, but because of his conviction of the enormous transformative resource for ministry that would otherwise have been neglected. His personal experience makes Hal an insightful guide for those who have also experienced or are contemplating an international immersion.

The third contribution of our guide on this journey is his persuasive analysis and biblical confirmation of the city as a central place in this process of globalization. Recinos understands God's mission plan for the church as humanizing our urbanized society, starting with the poor. The surprising size of the majority of those in North and Latin America who dwell in the cities grasps our attention. We are drawn by the author from the rural to the urban through his exploratory exegesis that takes us from the "perfect garden" of Genesis to Revelation's vision of the "perfect city." Recinos' refreshing portrait of the city is filled with hope, but never romanticized. The Bible is indeed about city-building with justice and equality. Travelers are reminded that we will not find the crucified God in the cultures of South or North unless we seek him in the ghettos.

Knowing Hal Recinos' dedication as a Bronx-born Puerto Rican to the Latino communities in the urban centers of North America, especially Washington, D.C. and New York, one might expect at least a flavor of Latino ethnocentrism in the presentation. The fourth contribution of this guide to applied globalization is Recinos' ability to hear and dialogue with other voices of liberation that occupy this sacred place of God's dwelling. Recinos acknowledges the powerful resources of the Latino community and the importance of identifying with a specific cultural community. However, he celebrates and explores issues of mutual learning with Jewish, black, womanist, and Native American communities. Hal challenges and motivates the church to be involved in networks of participatory and dialogical encounter as the essence of mission and ministry.

Fifth, this academically and theoretically competent exploration of globalization through immersion in the city is eminently practical. The final chapter leads travelers through the application of pastoral anthropology to an experience of local immersion. It takes the reader through the process of forming listening groups to appreciating the importance of dialogue partners and the mutuality of ecclesial renewal.

The sixth contribution of this work is implied by the holistic imagery of pastoral anthropology that calls one not only to local immersion in the city, but also to a consistent return to the global. Local immersions should motivate solidarity with the poor and the marginalized in Africa, Asia, Latin America, and Europe, as well as North America. Hal Recinos' involvement in the justice struggle of Salvadoran refugees in Washington, D.C. empowers his advocacy for systemic justice in Peru and South Africa. His activities illustrate the reciprocal dialogue between the local and global perspectives.

The final test of the importance of this work will be the degree of our response. If the scout's reports appear reliable and the guide's experience and analysis credible, the decision ought to be: Begin the journey. There will, of course, be byways and distractions. However, as Hal Recinos would affirm and I would confirm, it is the Holy Spirit working between us and among us in those encounters with radically different cultures that results in personal transformation and empowerment. The consequent challenge is to move from personal change to institutional, and even systems change. Pastor Recinos is profoundly aware of the need for a biblically-based global vision for both theological education and the ministry of the church. The isolation and provincialism of North American educational processes stifle the dialogue between North American Christians and those with a dynamic faith in different cultures. In a poetically enriched form, Hal Recinos calls us to the city to redress a lack of global awareness that impedes the realization of a vision of a more just and sustainable world community to which the Holy Spirit calls.

Robert A. Evans
Executive Director
Plowshares Institute

# BRINGING HOME THE MEANING OF GLOBALIZATION

Norht American Christians have become concerned with developing a global perspective on issues related to the practice of faith in the world. In the next century, Christian ethics in the United States cannot simply relate the world to North Atlantic systems of concern. Instead, persons of faith living in Caesar's household will seek deeper immersion in the reality of the world understood as a global village. The impact of an international perspective will contribute to the growing realization that the victims of the old self-interested North Atlantic order are leading the way toward the renewal of creation.

Globalization is being talked about at all levels of the church. North American Christians participating in globalization immersion experiences in Third World societies often return to home churches transformed by their encounter with the Crucified One in the oppressed and poor. Out of a deeply personal experience of metanoia, these persons opt to impact the structures of society that maintain life-denying systems that nourish selfish wealth. Some question the idea that personal transformation will lead toward social institutional restructuring in the long run; however, it must not be forgotten that globalization is a process in time that points to the importance of linking personal change with social activism.

Globalization has been a movement issuing forth from the compassionate ethics of a predominantly white middle class. The movement takes seriously the justice requirements of the gospel. This project in faith ethics has placed North American Christians in

# *Latino Town*

merengue music is being tapped
rhythmically by tired work feet,
drenching the hot sidewalk in sweat:

it's Latino town and the secondhand
cars, the third and fourth ones too,
are up on jacks being fixed and admired.

it doesn't make a difference on a sabado
afternoon. it's Latino town and grandmothers
are emerging from the tenements adopting whole

blocks, silently being everyone's abuelita.
it's Latino town and the hydrants are at full force;
scattered cans of Coke and beer are being

gathered by little children,
who run up to the old man selling piragua
to ask that he open the ends so they can spray

the water at each other, the buses, the
buildings and have a laugh, such a risa.
it's Latino town and at ten o'clock this morning

the Goya little league will begin to play against
Bustelo's little league, and it's beans against cafe
once again, they say. it's Latino town and Julia

and Tito have opened their first-floor window
real wide listening to the music they put on la
radiola while rehearsing the moves for tonight's big

baile. it's Latino town and in front of the bodega
sit Don Carlo, Don Pepe, Don Wilfredo, and Charly
on milk boxes emptied of treats, playing dominoes.

it's Latino town, and all the smiles are in
Spanish. . . .

solidarity with the justice and human rights struggles of the Third World poor. The importance of that kind of identification can never be overemphasized; however, globalization has failed to make connections with the poor of first world society who are overwhelmingly rooted in the inner cities of the nation. The concern for transformation has for the most part not moved middle-class Christians to identification with the vision of a renewed society held by Latinos, blacks, Asians, Arabs, Native Americans, and poor whites.

I once attended a meeting in which the impact of globalization on the individual was being discussed. The organizer was sharing how persons involved in immersion projects "come back" profoundly transformed by their experiences. This globalization organizer was trying to convince me that an encounter with the oppressed overseas was going to change me in a profound way. Encountering God in the existential reality of the poor and oppressed overseas certainly has profound consequences for any Christian. I was most taken by the apparent blindness to the possibility of that encounter at home. The North American Latino experience, in which I share, was not part of the organizer's globalization vocabulary or personal immersion experience.

North American Latinos are instruments of globalization for white society. Christians need to link their concern for developing an international perspective to the reality of the poor and Latino community within its own borders. The progressive church of established white society needs to seek the immersion of the city. Seeking God in the city means encountering the Crucified One in the faces of the nation's poor and oppressed. Globalization into the next millennium entails incarnating God's word in the context of the barrio by learning what it means to face the reality of international economics from ghetto apartments and violent streets.

In the sixteenth century, international economics gave rise to a form of labor based on the enslavement of Africans and Native Americans who produced the wealth of the North Atlantic world. Neo-colonialism in the nineteenth century produced global economic structures no less dependent on exploiting labor outside of the North Atlantic world. Subsequently, third world society saw the creation of a mass of exploited classes, as well as the displacement of persons to the North Atlantic world. Today, African Americans, Native Americans, Latinos, and Asians are the struggle-laden children of the international political economy—an economic system born five hundred years ago. These children of oppression in the new world continue to live at the margins of society in the ghettos and barrios of the nation. Their labor is yet exploited to benefit a financial system that excludes them from real possibilities of life.

It is my hope that this work will contribute to the process of bringing home the meaning of globalization. This work speaks out of the particularity of the Latino experience in the United States. Attempts at generalizing about the experiences of other ethnic groups reflects a spirit of dominance which I do not share. References to non-Latinos in this work are made in relation to the concern for telling the Latino story. A spirit of exclusion does not underlie the focus on the Latino experience in the United States. My hope is that the insights rooted in the singular experiences of this invisible Latino community can be used by church persons interested in globalization.

Nevertheless, globalization as the mutual interpretation of ecclesial tradition and missional practice will not only be considered in light of the mission of the Latino church, but other ethnic/womanist discourse will also be discussed. The black, womanist, Latino, Arab, and Native American church traditions point to a nonracist, nonclassist, nonsexist, pro-communitarian and pro-creation appropriation of God's Word. To be sure, the goal of all distressed communities in the United States should be to establish round-table discussions at the local, regional, and national levels to give each other hope and courage to create changed conditions of life.

Each community would speak out of its singular experience in a context of dialogue directed toward creating an authentic justice-oriented people in solidarity. Globalization is a way to renew the ministry and mission of the church. This work only seeks to add the long-muted voice of Latinos in North American society given the intellectual and ethical preoccupations of white and black society. First, chapter 1 provides an image of aspects of life in the barrio. I invite the reader in this chapter to begin the process of globalization by entering the reality of the barrio. Poems will be used throughout the book to facilitate the reader's entrance into barrio and urban reality. The collection of social, political, religious, and economic commentary poetry will enable the reader to view life in the barrio from below.

Chapter 2 examines global and urban themes in the scriptural tradition indicating how the city is reported in the Bible to be one of God's sacred spaces. Chapter 3 will invite the reader to ponder the rise of globalization in the decade of the eighties in terms of reconsidering the role of the city for the internationalizing process. Chapter 4 examines the meaning of globalization understood as an encounter

# *Mother*

it was many years ago in what
seems ages forgotten covered over

by the sands of time and buried deep
inside that a woman made in the image

of hope left an island—Puerto Rico—
called home. wandering through the still

city streets beneath crumbling tenements
beside broken dreamers became her fate

embraced in the new land as the cracks
around a heart that love seldom filled

grew in pain. time ran for the hills each
day a new burden was given birth in a

world that never could say her name. then,
came an infant's heart to fill with tender

love through mother's eyes badly beaten by
a man's rage. the child spawned never lived

the meaning of home nor the woman the feeling
of mother. each day devoted to labor in a

textile factory of the city pushed dreams
of a better life far away into an unreachable

unreachable . . . unreachable . . . horizon.

with black, Arab, Native American, and feminist/womanist realities. Close attention will be given to the particular gifts to Christianity made by these traditions.

Chapter 5 explores ways in which globalization in the context of North American society might become a reality for the local church. Globalization takes cultural contexts seriously for the task of doing theology and renewing the church. This section will examine the contributions anthropology can make to the enterprise of globalization. Chapter 6 surveys anthropological approaches to cultural immersion. Ethnographic methods aim to examine the totality of social experience to facilitate self-knowledge. Thus, readers will be given useful suggestions regarding how to develop understandings of ministry from the perspective of "Pastoral Anthropology."

# CHAPTER ONE

# IMAGES OF THE CITY

My parents arrived in the United States impassioned by a dream of making it in a land of opportunity. What they found was quite different. Their story, like that of so many Latinos who arrived on these shores or whose land was taken in the period of nineteenth-century expansion to the Southwest and Puerto Rico, is one of broken dreams and poverty. My parents remained foreigners in the United States. They never moved beyond the structures that established white society left them in the inner city of New York. Poverty and racial discrimination were central aspects of their Latino experience in established white society. They were welcomed as a source of cheap and exploitable labor that created the wealth of the nation.

Puerto Rican first-generation Latinos, sometimes known as Nuyoricans, are heirs to their parent's history of marginalization. For many, that history is one of oppression and untimely death. I am the first "kid" from my own neighborhood to have gone back to school after dropping out and to have graduated from high school. Out of a group of ten close childhood friends, five have died unnatural deaths, one is in the Navy, and the others are either heroin addicts or in jail, or both. In the Latino community in the United States, my story is not an exception. The reality of my people is harsh and bitter, dark and cold like a winter night in the South Bronx. It is a reality where people struggle and struggle and struggle ad infinitum.

Factory wages and a divorce meant that my mother would not be able to raise the three kids for which she gained custody. She lost two sons to the streets of the South Bronx. We became junkies. Shooting dope was the ultimate concern of our lives. Yet, on the street I discovered the God who knows the suffering and death of human beings dismissed by established society. For me, God was present in the street experience of utter abandonment. God incarnate in Jesus was in my very flesh as a homeless child who searched for food in restaurant garbage cans, shelter in abandoned tenements, and who wore the same clothes for months at a time.

## LAUNDROMAT FOR JUNKIES

I used to hang out in a laundromat on Home Street. There, the God of the oppressed existed in the sorrow of homeless junkies dangling from a thread of life. In the laundromat God's Word takes flesh in worn junkie faces that reflect the time-carved wretchedness of Golgotha. I remember the laundromat as the center of the universe that received rejected human beings who entered to escape winter and life in the barrio. We told each other stories while community residents washed clothes. Our shared junkie stories were so similar in essential detail that only distortion of the biographical facts assured the preservation of a separate and unique identity.

My brother Rudy was part of the laundromat crowd. He lived just across the street in one of the tenements that had long been abandoned to junkies by a landlord. It was here that he retreated to find solitude and shed grim tears. In his dark room, candlelight would illuminate memories. He wondered if he had ever been tenderly embraced while a child, if he had ever truly been loved. Rudy shared with me that he always tried to silence these thoughts; his mind preferred to return to the pit of his personal junkie prison. Only the next day's fix and the afternoon at the laundromat deserved emotional attention in the dark stillness of his one-room apartment in an abandoned building.

Often, Rudy wondered how many more muggings he could successfully do before getting caught? How many young mothers' welfare checks and food stamps would he be able to steal before the Catholic Latino God let judgment fall upon him? I often wondered how long Rudy could live in the darkness of a room that resembled the garbage that lay on the city streets? Only dope and a cheap wine called "Night Train" seemed to provide answers for Rudy and those like him.

# A Junkie's Daughter

standing on the corner in her
father's grip she wants to run
far away from the tracks that

make his heart stone. he surfaces
from time to time to tell someone
his name forming barely audible words

whose sounds remind him of the
eleven-year-old child beside him
and Papo killed last night for a

cheap radio. his head shakes
to each side expressing a small
recognition of horror at the

thought of death in the streets
then such feelings fade away
barely able to find shape and

form in his junkie heart for very
long. the daughter still struggles
to be free of the junkiedom ruling

life that banishes her
father to a nameless kingdom
that crushes everything in sight.

In the laundromat I discovered that junkie agony subordinates all things to itself. The fellowship of junkies opens a limited and limiting world to interior horizons that are seldom consciously experienced. Dope and booze allowed the junkies in the laundromat to find form in an insane world, history in voicelessness, identity in anonymity, and life in death.

Everyone who enters a laundromat in the barrio is at once actor and audience. Life as a performance was celebrated each day in my hangout with all the conviction of a Christian revival meeting. I recollect the afternoon that Carlos came in with a Calvin Klein suit he had stolen from a store on Fordham Road. He tried it on while standing behind an industrial dryer—his fitting room. He planned to wear it to his sister's wedding. It was too big for his skinny junkie body. He smiled, looking down at the jacket sleeves completely covering both hands. Now he would not have to miss the wedding for lack of suitable clothes to wear. He said, "Pass the Night Train, bros." Laundromats in the South Bronx are life's stage.

Junkie life is largely about waiting to get a high or to get off dope. I was in the laundromat the day Rudy inspired me to write the poem, "Been Waiting." Let me tell you what happened. Rudy felt it was time to move. He was feeling restless for the calming embrace of dope. Junkies are always on the move. "Yo, see youse later," he said. We departed. Out on the cold street winter smacked us in the face like a hawk snatches its prey. Rudy commented on how grateful he was for the rubber boots he had found in yesterday's garbage can. They not only covered his feet, but also protected him against their foul odor.

## THE SHOOTING GALLERY

We walked past the liquor store and beyond the subway station toward "the block." Somehow that term always struck me more as a prison reference than a place where people lived. Soon Rudy was scratching the tracks on his arms anticipating the dope to be found on "the block." Our pace quickened as each step carried us closer to that moment of joy caused by the rush of dope in human blood. Junkies were everywhere on "the block." They were scattered about the streets waiting for something to happen to them and for them. We were excited that soon we would enact our most beloved ritual of despair.

# Been Waiting

Rudy's waiting on the corner for his
big hit. he's been waiting now for ten years
and the tracks in his arms
where Señora Heroina does come quiets

him for the wait while promising a
more complete destiny someday. he's
been waiting for the lover he
dreams of, for bitterness to run away,

for a blade of grass to grow from the
crack in the sidewalk that he stares
at in the wait, for Orchard Beach

to be in his pocket so he can reach in
for a calm feel to living; he's been waiting
for the welfare check, for the roaches to
take a walk from his one room where there

ain't no food no way. he's been waiting to
kick a jones he doesn't have, for his mother
who long ago said good-bye, for his country to

be born in him. he's been waiting for Lelo, who
left the waiting corner to join the navy and kick
his brothers' asses down in Vieques under orders

just to live. he's been waiting for spring and summer
and fall and forget about winter because
the corner is cold. he's been waiting for the

right time of day or night to think about
waiting some more.

Only the ritual of shooting heroin permits junkies to think tirelessly about new life that never seems to come.

Rudy looked around for his connection. El Viejo (the old man) would always give my brother a couple of bags of dope in exchange for some customers. Perhaps, my brother earned the name "the Mayor" on the block precisely because he was a good salesman. Even junkies must work. "Hey man, what's up?" Rudy asked El Viejo. Rudy was asked by the connection to find dope customers and bring them over to the waiting corner. "Brother Rudy, you know the deal. I'm gonna be over on the corner. Bring the dope fiends down," said El Viejo. Four customers later the connection handed Rudy two ten-dollar bags of dope. They had a perfect relationship defined by a remarkable lack of confusion regarding the division of labor. Street society has a division of labor just like established society.

Street preachers are often found on corners exhorting junkies and community residents. My poem entitled "Them Preachers" was partly suggested to me by a female street preacher Rudy and I passed on the way to a shooting gallery. The preacher wore a white dress, the uniform of an evangelical.[1] God had commanded her not to wear facial cosmetics or pants and to give Caesar all her loyalty and obedience in worldly things. She was standing on the street corner happy to have received a permit to hold a public hearing and preach. This country was great because it gave her freedom of speech. She was exercising that freedom on barrio corners under the shadow of an American flag and in the company of a tapping tambourine.

A small crowd had gathered around this fiery preacher. The crowd of barrio poor who gathered were in need of a liberating word; however, the woman's words merely accused the listeners of sinfulness, of succumbing to the influence of Satan and of being the cause of their own miserable historical experience. The will of God meant judgment! The preacher's message depicted a savior not interested in taking people's hands and escorting them to a new encounter with justice and fairness in society. Instead, she spoke of a Christian experience rooted in a vision of the church loyal to the white establishment in America and restricted to the actual conditions of life in the slums.

We reached the shooting gallery. Barbara ran it out of her apartment on Longfellow Avenue. She was one of the few black persons who did not move once Puerto Ricans began to live in the neighborhood. Barbara was a longtime community resident who was part of an earlier migration of blacks that caused the Italians, Irish, and Jews to move to suburban communities. She loved to shoot dope.

# *Them Preachers*

we got preachers down here
been making big promises about plates
always filled with our rice and beans:
we will never starve or wonder what the

right word was or wasn't that lost us
the welfare check down at the social services
where all them gringo christians are for us
to feed themselves on lawned homes in suburbia where

God is lily-white and children pray to jesus via
IBM, IT&T, EXXON, and giddy-up on we; and
we keep hearing about the Jones Act of 1917 that
made us citizens of tenements in spanglish town
with rats for pets and toilets that hardly flush

they say are better than the latrines we left
at home that General Miles claimed with el retorico
of freedom and christian democratic civility. Yes,
we are citizens and free! the churches close the
gates to heaven except from 9-5 and Sunday because

the junkies want the gold crucifix to get a fix
themselves; Yes, we are citizens and free! there
goes pretty Rosa on her way to Simpson Street to
hustle men who still have jobs and wives long left
in Brooklyn; Yes, we are citizens and free! and its

graduation day for those who made it through the
sixth grade then, the ninth. they can't read yet
but their mothers are proud of them pieces of paper
that will get them jobs in factories with bosses who
see in them the sweat that makes the rich; Yes, we

are citizens and free! and the preacher keeps telling
us about jesu cristo with an american flag hung on the
crumbling wall behind him reading an RSV—english—while
latino refugees walk past on the other side of the road
thinking to be free; Yes, what was that, we are citizens
and free!

Prostitution on Simpson Street was not for her. Her hands were too deformed and repulsive from all the years of shooting dope to appeal to "johns." Those injured hands insinuated another time when forebears were beaten and killed by the institution of slavery. Dope was yet a new form of slavery creating wealth by disfiguring the lives of people in the ghetto.

A profound feeling of excitement overcomes you just before you prepare to shoot dope. Your mind is consumed by the thought of placing the needle into a vein and watching blood rush into the eyedropper mixing with the dope solution that is injected directly into the red stream. The "fix" expels chills, cramps, clamminess, paranoia, and all feelings of utter isolation in street junkies. I recollect that after a "fix" Barbara's hands always appeared less ugly, the South Bronx was not moving toward death, and childhood memories had a quality of joy denied them by actuality. For us, freedom was at the end of a needle assuring historical being of a new deportment defined by impassivity. Ours was the freedom of living in death.

We knocked on Barbara's door. We were escorted into the living room of the apartment where a candle's flame danced on a coffee table in the middle of the room. Barbara's "old man" was nodding out on the sofa lost in the world of junkiedom. Barbara walked toward the rear of the apartment and returned with the "works," the needles and eyedroppers necessary for shooting dope. We took the "works" and gave her a user's fee of five dollars and proceeded to carefully open the two "dime" bags of dope. Once the bags were opened, Rudy poured their contents into a bottle cap that had a bobby pin placed around it to form a handle as on a small cooking pot. Junkies refer to this device as "the cooker." Rudy added half an eyedropper of water to the dope in "the cooker" and held a match beneath it.

Three matches were always used for best results. Junkies are trinitarians. The ritual of heroin was about to be completed. Rudy wrapped a belt around his arm to expose the veins. The needle was guided to the place on his arm that would numb all the pain. Rudy felt good and free. We were happy now. I remember sitting in Barbara's dimly lighted apartment observing the dancing flame and feeling a deep silence come over me. Dope makes you stop thinking or feeling the wretched memories and experience of poverty. Junkiedom means doing time beyond the conditions of ordinary existence. Nothing matters but dope and the obsessively sought-after nod.

## THE BLOCK: A GLOBAL MEETING GROUND

Nevertheless, for me the larger meaning of "the block" was rooted in precious memories granting life genuine meaning. Those memories were about more than the wretchedness of junkiedom. The block was a humanly diverse reality during part of my experience, before the heroin plague. The South Bronx was truly an urban context for global encounter. Will Lee's mother ran the neighborhood Chinese hand laundry, a storefront synagogue sat on the corner, East European Jews ran candy stores and merchandise shops, Italians owned restaurants, the Irish and blacks worked in the factories alongside Puerto Ricans. These groups would gather in a little park to listen to conga players on summer nights who drummed sounds that originated in Africa.

Any summer evening one could hear the rhythmic beauty of congas floating in the air on "the block." The drumming pierced even the bitterest of hearts and transported them to spaces of dreams. Life in the South Bronx was lived with the help of congas. People poured out of their buildings on conga nights entranced by the beats and skipped beats of the drummers. The little park and "the block" were no more than the context of village life in the heart of urban reality. Life on "the block" was about unity, but also of children growing up together, quitting school together, going hungry, homeless, getting hooked on dope, landing in jail, hating and dying, all together.

On "the block" Puerto Ricans discovered that the God brought to them by North American missionaries was historically impotent in the city. Puerto Ricans turned to their non-Western God in the South Bronx. Many enslaved Africans who were brought to Puerto Rico to labor in place of the dying native peoples were Yoruba. Their traditional religion persisted under the conditions of oppressive slavery and imposed colonial Christianity. The Yoruba influenced Puerto Rican culture especially in the form of worship to the Yoruban God, Chango. I used to attend "espiritista" (African Chango-based spiritualism) meetings with my friend Joseph and his mother on Friday evenings in the South Bronx.

Joseph's mother Cuca was a very short woman. She walked with a slight forward lean and, though she was a permanent member of "the block," she managed to keep a distance from its affairs. She was a deeply religious woman, but not in the Christian orthodox sense. Religion to her was not merely that which took place on Sunday at the local Catholic church—Saint John's Chrysostom Church. Religion did not mean putting on a Sunday personality and taking a friendly stroll through the neighborhood nor was it a primarily personal experience with God in heaven. Religion was not an act, an outer-skin to be shed for the work week, or an exercise in conformity by participation in ritual affairs.

For Cuca, religion was an event where humanity encountered manifestations of God incarnate as Chango. Religion meant leaving the world of poverty for a context where one pulled the strings like some priestess and spoke with God or the devil. For Cuca religion was about finding the power denied to her in the social reality of daily life as a Puerto Rican woman. Worship of Chango gave her a way to construct an alternative and empowering reality. She discovered a kind of freedom in Chango. Local priests from the Catholic church mostly thought of dismantling Chango worship. They failed to recognize that belief in this Yoruban God for Puerto Ricans was ritual connected to altering the terrain of oppression in the context of the South Bronx and white society.

Joseph's mother worked all day in New York's garment district. Her morning began at seven to the sounds of radio WADO, the Latino broadcast station. On the weekends Cuca would spend time with her son Joseph who lived with his father. She had divorced her first husband and had given up custody of their child but retained weekend visitation rights. Cuca believed in the power of ritual manipulation of historical uncertainty and the unknown future. Fridays were very special days for Cuca. Her son always stayed with her and they would visit the "espiritista" (Chango Spiritualist). In the South Bronx there are many storefront "espiritista" meeting halls where African gods and Catholic myths are joined to construct definitions of existence that envisage the end of oppressed-suffering.

Espiritista meeting halls are designed like the standard church pattern. An altar is located at the front of the space on which icons of African and Christian divinities are placed. Candles burn constantly before the images. The people light them in order to gain a favor. I remember that the meeting room was always crowded. More women and children than men attended sessions. Mystery consumed the space and consoled all who entered it with a genuine need to find answers to life that made sense. I attended an unforgettable espiritista meeting one Friday evening with Joseph and his mother. Ritual actors danced that night in the meeting hall beside the altar. They called the ancient spirits to the wretchedness of South Bronx Puerto Rican souls.

I sat in the back of the espiritista meeting hall with Joseph that memorable evening. We laughed about all the foolish ritual of the adult world. A silence fell over the room overtaking everyone present with a feeling of elevated expectation. A light from a back room shone over the center of the floor before the altar area. All the eyes in the room fell upon that very spot. The door from which the light was projected slowly opened creating a bright single lane on the floor. A woman appeared. Everyone watched her intently. She was the priestess. A male drummer followed her into the room playing the music that would conjure up Chango—the giver of all future insight and hope.

The drummer called the spirit world, while the priestess made her body a medium of communication. Each note played by the drummer seemed to contain a piece of the Puerto Rican dream of making it. The little park had moved indoors; however, the drummer created a sound quite unlike the festive beats common to the public fair of the little park. He played slowly, as if petting the drum skins. The rhythm inspired a sense of awe in the gathered people. Only the drum could be heard at first, then after one last slap of the drumskin all fell silent. Meanwhile, the woman who entered the room with the drummer, the priestess, had lit a cigar and placed it in her mouth. She took a puff from the cigar and walked to the center of the room.

Soon the drum began to chant again. The priestess was transforming before all the once-disbelieving eyes. She threw her head back and jerked it around, violently. As she bent her torso forward, she would, again, throw her head around her shoulders as if she meant to throw it to some distant part of the meeting hall. Her entire body trembled as she fell to the floor. It appeared she was unconscious; but her eyes were wide open and a fit of convulsion was consuming her. The drummer continued to play almost unaware of what was happening in front of him. His job was to play the drum, nothing else.

From the front row of seats a very old African-Puerto Rican woman pulled a tambourine out of a shopping bag and began to play. As she played she sang: "Que viva Chango!—Long live Chango!" Now the others in the room joined in the worship cry. A god was being worshipped. Not the helpless God imaged by the crucifix that hangs in the local Catholic church that is resigned to suffering on a cross, but God disguised in the memory of African humanity enfleshed by poor Puerto Ricans. The priestess's body stopped convulsing and order seemed to be returning to it. As she got up off the floor she reached over and grabbed the cigar that lay beside her. She took a long puff, inhaling smoke, endowing the very act with holy attendance.

The priestess began talking. What everyone heard that Friday evening was a man's voice speaking through a woman's body. Only

31

Chango was in the room. I overheard a couple of young women express fear about the devil taking advantage of the moment by possessing the old lady with the tambourine in order to bring ill-fate to all nearby. Others assured them that Chango was too powerful for the Western devil. No evil would befall them while in the presence of the God of power and truth. The room and everyone in it had become Chango's own. The people were part of a liturgy celebrating the absolute power of an African deity who had traveled from West Africa, interpenetrated the history of Puerto Ricans and resurrected in the barrio.

The priestess stopped dancing. A new stage in the ritual event of divinization was reached. She walked up and down the aisle proclaiming the name of Chango, and blowing clouds of smoke from the cigar into the faces of selected persons. Chango danced in the mist. Chango called a Louis Colon to the altar. A small commotion was heard coming from the back of the room as a rather short man walked down the aisle. Chango blew smoke into his face. Louis began to cry before Chango who promised to bring prosperity to Mr. Colon's life. Chango freed Louis in that singular moment from the unhalting grind of daily struggle with conditions of poverty that even hard work never overcame.

Louis returned to his seat. The drum began to play again. The priestess moved toward us. Chango was about to speak to us. The priestess's eyes, the eyes of Chango, fell on us. Joseph stared directly into Chango's eyes which had layers of power. I have never forgotten the words uttered by the priestess during that encounter with Joseph. "Joseph," said Chango, "you don't believe what you have just seen. You are very young and this seems like a game, but you will remember these words spoken tonight. You will die on a rooftop on your eighteenth birthday, alone. You laugh but remember what you have been told." Joseph did not believe a word of the divinization. The priestess was just another South Bronx hustler living on the suffering and needs of the poor.

The priestess blew another cloud of smoke from the cigar. She addressed me, "Harold, your future will be unstable for years to come. There is an evil spirit and I will protect you from it. Remember, the bad years will come and they will pass bringing with their death good ones. Expect me with you." Naturally, each word uttered by Chango seemed too absurd to me as well. Joseph and I were left in a world of confusion and doubt as the priestess returned to the front of the room. What had occurred between us was beyond immediate explanation; however, years later Joseph, in fact, died alone on a rooftop at the age of eighteen, and my life as an adolescent junkie who lived on the streets for several years yielded to better days.

The drummer began to play faster and faster as the priestess returned to the original dance which had started the evening's ritual. The front of the room was a cloud of smoke. Through it the priestess's head swayed from side to side in a frenzy as the dance became more physical. She fell to the floor. Silence filled the room once more. She lay motionless. The people grew restless. People wanted something else to happen. The crowd at the back of the room stirred trying to get a look. She began to move and the drummer went over to help her up. The ritual event was officially over. The players exited through the door leading to a back room. The house lights were turned up and ushers began collecting the expected donations.

On the streets, however, I encountered the God of life at the margins (Matthew 25:31-46). Christ was in the experience of utter abandonment I came to know so well on the streets. Christ came to me in the flesh of priests from Saint John's Chrysostom Church in the South Bronx. From them, I first learned about the Christian faith, in the tears shed on lonely nights in barrio tenements, and in the person of a white Presbyterian minister and his family who nurtured me back to life from junkiedom. I will not tell you that my life in Christ changed suddenly; instead, I now know that Christ has never abandoned me—even in my most difficult time of suffering. Through my life experience, I came to understand that Christ was calling me to view the margins of human existence as a place of hope that yearns for justice and love. Christ was in my poverty leading me to become a minister devoted to understanding how the poor and oppressed interpret what is ultimate for Christianity.

## MANHATTAN: THE GLOBAL ISLAND

Christianity on Home Street provided people with an otherworldly hope and language. Chango religion nurtured a spirituality related to their material struggle against conditions of concrete oppression. Still, junkies lived in an altogether other world. Their world celebrates moments. Junkies experience security in the perishing moments found in an hour, day, week, or neatly ordered year. Junkies participate in historical time with utter abandonment because for them life is nonexistence and nonpersonhood. For junkies, time is nodding out once high, daily suffering, and the joint (jail). For junkies time is the measure of all promises about getting off dope that never come in time.

Extreme poverty on "the block" was evidenced in the wasteland of street corner junkies and the reality of family fragmentation in people's lives. For me, shooting dope made wretched existence sufferable. Living on the streets for several years resulted in my having to drop out of junior high school. Street life became my ultimate concern and teacher. To be a junkie meant each day was primarily centered on surviving and getting high. Many junkie friends were dead from overdoses or murdered on the street. I managed to survive one stabbing. Childhood had come to an abrupt end for me on streets where I begged for money, searched garbage cans for food, hardly ever changed my clothing, and slept wherever possible on the streets.

Someone I met on the street maintained a one-room apartment on the Lower East Side of Manhattan. Occasionally, I would spend nights in that space listening to the sounds of the street which always managed to transport me to "the block." I thought of Simpson Street were Rosa was hustling mostly Latino "tricks," the BBQ chicken joint around which junkies, pill-heads, prostitutes, and the working class congregated each night with drunks barely able to walk after a night in the corner bar. Memories of a shoot-up buddy named Hank who supported his habit by stealing the copper plumbing pipes from abandoned tenements often broke into my intense feeling of solitude in that room.

My first encounter with the global character of the city occurred on the Lower East Side of Manhattan. During simple walks in the neighborhood, I remember hearing Russian, Polish, German, Italian, Yiddish, Japanese, Chinese, Arabic, Spanish, English, and Hindi, among other languages. Stores, cafés, and restaurants were run by diverse groups who enjoyed sharing their cultural cuisine, material cultural products, customs, opinions, and plain conversation. A few Jewish theater groups still maintained vibrant life. Coffeehouses were obviously contexts for debating politics and social concerns from different cultural perspectives and in light of larger global realities.

I never imagined someday returning to the Lower East Side to serve a first pastoral appointment in a United Methodist Church. Faith directed a Presbyterian minister to activate God's love on the streets of the barrio by engaging in the struggle of society's rejects. Because Ken Haines and his family traversed a road less traveled and dared to have a global encounter by entering the world of a Puerto Rican junkie, my

# Christmas on the Rooftops

beneath the rooftop on which
the Ukrainians sing worn smiles
on pedestrian faces signal the

joy of the season. the smell of
of pine paves its way on the
neighborhood streets enveloping

the faint sighs issuing forth
from the mouths of street people
for whom the odor commands a parade

of memory that points to another time
and life. nativity scenes are in most
of the shop windows each expressing

another cultural face of this place.
down the street in the little park
another group sings the hymns that

announce in song the imminent birth
rendered in the lyrics of a by-gone
victorian day yet a small crowd has gathered

to hear the words so far away from life
it seems but calling. now, the newspaper
trucks are arriving over which the singing

voices seem to shout only to slowly
fall into a curious silence.

life turned out differently and I became a minister.² Drug addiction had caused me to move all about New York City, Los Angeles, and San Juan, Puerto Rico. Every move involved an attempt to overcome my bondage to dope, but I always discovered where to buy heroin in each city.

Life with a white family from the United States convinced me that globalization was about mutual historical interpretation of racial and cultural experiences. My life passages were products of globalization beginning with the dynamics that caused working-class parents to migrate North from neocolonial societies under the hegemony of the United States; the system of marginalization in established white society that gave birth to the Latino ghetto; the massive heroin trade of the 1960s and 1970s caused by increased drug traffic during the Vietnam War; and the encounter between white and Latino society that took place in the Haines household.

Once off dope and back in school, I had to struggle with a great many issues related to my disconnection with my biological family and life in another cultural and racial reality. My new family walked with me toward a new understanding of social being in a society that needed greater levels of solidarity and dialogue between radically different groups. In seminary, biblical stories of transformation and the city captured my imagination and directed me toward the idea of going into ministry. I knew from experience that the broken, the oppressed, the poor, the sick, the elderly, women, sojourners, and all such persons found in large numbers in the city are special in the sight of God.

My course work simply reconvinced me that faith can best be understood from the perspective of the real life struggles of persons who are already excluded from the fullness of life by marginating economic, political, racial, and cultural realities. I accepted an appointment to the Church of All Nations—Spanish on the Lower East Side of Manhattan. Through members of this largely Puerto Rican church my faith deepened and my commitment to the struggle of the city's underside grew stronger. Rudy lived with me for periods of time, but I was unable to help him give up his heroin and alcohol addictions. He died on April 7, 1985, Easter Sunday, on the very streets that had robbed him of life at the tender age of thirteen.³

I am convinced that globalization means the mutual encounter between persons from radically different worlds who choose to engage in a process of accompaniment directed toward empowerment for fullness in life. For me the city is God's sacred place precisely because it is a creative and cosmopolitan meeting ground for people. Urban reality makes plain the vigor of cultural communities; the meaning of concentrated economic and technological power; the importance of diverse racial and ethnic groups; the heart of nation-state governments; the struggle of race, class, gender, and culture; and the vision of Hebrew-Christian religion for the city yet to come.

Here let it be said that theology in the context of the city must make it clear to the faith community that God's promise of a new heaven and new earth implies developing a global perspective of humanity. For the church, globalization in the United States must mean enabling despised humanity to discover the power to change wretched conditions of life. This power comes from the gospel in the heart of the city and the life of the poor and exploited members of established society. Surely, globalization means the church will witness to God-in-Jesus Christ by promoting a reorganization of historical experience in society from the existential reality of those below.

I discovered the mystery of God's incarnation in the poor while living on Home Street in the South Bronx and the streets of various urban centers. I learned to view my world as a "Nuyorican" (U.S.-born Puerto Rican) poet. The reader will find poems in each chapter of this book that communicate feelings and images of life in the city as part of the experience of globalization. The poems also portray aspects of life in the barrio. Let me conclude by urging the reader to understand that God has formulated a mission plan for the church that requires followers of Christ to humanize our urbanizing world, beginning with the poor and oppressed of the nation's cities. Chapter 2 will now focus on the question of the Bible and the city.

## *Mama Dios*

dawn in New York unveils the brick
of tenements on streets holding the
withdrawing rays of a fading moon on

their corners. the pigeons begin
to stir for another fight of day
and the all too familiar streetwalker

negotiates a trick beneath the rising
light of sun. another sky patched with
clouds blue and full of stoic benediction

escorts all the corners of the city
through its sighs of hope for the
beloved people that together build

life. dawn in New York reveals the
evening tears of refugees exiled from
home sleeping to dream of tropical nights

covered with warm breezes and the grace
of evening sounds found despite the
horror of war. dawn in New York reminds

us that Mama Dios lives in the factories
now and the dreams remain the dreams while
the day invites to work. . . .

# CHAPTER TWO

# GOD'S SACRED PLACE:
## The City

Some 4.7 billion people exist in the world today. Forty percent of the global population lives in urban areas, while 61 percent of all Latin Americans and 75 percent of all North Americans live in urban areas.[1] Christians who confront the reality of urbanization quickly learn that suffering humanity determines what is ultimate for the church. By ultimate, I mean the starting point of ethical concern understood as the moral imperative of doing justice to the oppressed-poor as the first step of knowledge of God. The requirements of the gospel heard in the cries of abused persons call humanity to the struggle for justice. People from different parts of the world gather each day to fashion their lives in cities; hence, God calls the church to discover the meaning of globalization in the city.

The phenomenon of city-building implies a gathering of diverse people in a concentrated geographical area organized into a new life-style. Cities are vital centers of society because they nourish development and an increasing awareness of human social, political, economic, racial, and cultural diversity. Globalization as the encounter in urban space with human diversity is part of the life-style of the city. To be sure, the biblical witness itself not only records the process of city-building or urbanization, but also describes the way diverse human groups gathered in urban space to form new life together based on a system of justice and equality.

In our cities crack houses and street corners bare the mystery of God's incarnation in crucified humanity. God knows the oppression of the poor and rejected racial members of society in the city. God suffers with the people captive of the so-called "Crack Nation," who are crushed daily by the violence and politics of drugs. From the city God orders an end to injustice, crushing poverty, daily dehumanization, and the structural violence that keeps masses of poor people dislocated from economic and political power. Doubtless, the church as a historical agent of God is summoned to accompany the urban poor in their struggle for justice and equity in society.

God becomes flesh on the rooftops and in the crumbling tenements in places like the South Bronx, East Los Angeles, or Southeast Washington, D.C. Junkies and crack heads practice despair in those places by getting high on dope. God feels the pain of the mothers of the urban world who bury their children each day in the cemeteries of the nation's cities. God breathes the stale air of forsaken streets that have become home to countless families who have been sent to the margins of society. The crucified God can be found among the nation's growing numbers of poor on food lines. Jesus rises with the crucified humanity of the city waiting for his church to fulfill its mission of delivering good news and the fullness of life.

The church is called to the city to live out the terms of its covenant. God wants to be found in the logic of ghetto suffering—the reasoned system of life or social structure responsible for the organization of painful human experience in the ghettos and barrios. Such suffering is often explained quite logically by established society through an ideology that "blames the victim." For instance, the poor suffer because they are too lazy to work, they deal drugs because they lack moral character, and so forth. The logic of ghetto suffering is constituted in part by the system of reasoning that justifies subhuman existence as the natural product of the poor.

Already, the crucified Lord speaks out of the silence of young black and Latino men who are murdered in the nation's ghettos in drug deals and random urban violence. God opposes how established society treats their death with ordinariness. The structure of urban violence points back to an indifferent society that never bothers to ask the names of the dead. God wears the suffering faces of the children and the elderly who fearfully walk the urban streets. Only a church that loves the trampled neighbor of the ghetto can claim to have authentic love for God in a world of little compassion (see 1 John 3:17, 18).

Reality is the aspect of existence that the church must come to examine more closely. God calls the church to urban reality to engage in activity aimed at the structural transformation of society by embodying the principles of justice and love. God labors with the

# Saturday South Bronx Noon

two o'clock sabado afternoon
the streets have been still all
morning but now the faces begin pouring

like rain out of buildings onto the
avenue for a day of labor or getting
over on each other. nothing has changed

in this place where the living sigh
of dying years on end. they say the Ricans
once had jobs but work now cannot be

found that the factories have left
to starve latinos on penny-wages just
South of the border. dark is the language

of the streets where the churches have
erected heaven on promises never kept
and gates placed on building steps to keep

the junkies out. terror is the language
of the day the cops body dropped Bobby
on the corner that marks the grieving of

his wife. sabado afternoon and the workers,
those still employed downtown, are thinking
about pushing coat racks along seventh avenue

next week wondering about the meaning
of opportunity in the land of freedom
that grows sugarcane so bitter today.

humanity cast aside by established society in the city. Jesus weeps with the marginalized and poor humanity of the urban world, providing courage and hope to those who struggle to radically transform their mutilating social order. Urban reality summons the church to respond to the structure of dehumanization and inequality defining the life of the poor and oppressed. The church as bearer of the good news of Jesus Christ is asked to opt for the urban marginated classes by healing their brokenness.

## GOD'S GLOBAL CONTEXT: THE CITY

The Bible lands cover a vast area extending from India to Spain, and from southern Russia to south Arabia.[2] Cities are central to the scriptural witness; yet, the Bible has largely been read as a collection of antiurban writings. Many Christians viewing the canonical tradition from such a perspective believe God is primarily concerned with rural people. God expresses a different word in the biblical record. The totality of the created order is sacred for God; however, urban space is undeniably one of God's leading sacred places. The Bible is not only quite pro-urban, but, for contemporary humanity the city is the concrete context of the divine plan of salvation where God promises: "I am with you always, to the end of the age" (Matthew 28:20).

God's drama of salvation history begins in a perfect garden (Genesis 1) and progresses toward the vision of a perfect city (Revelation 22). Jesus revealed himself as a liberator in the city of Nazareth where he proclaimed "good news to the poor. . . . release to the captives . . . sight to the blind, to set at liberty those who are oppressed and to proclaim the acceptable year of the Lord" (Luke 4:18-19, RSV). In Jesus Christ humanity enters into a renewed salvific relationship with God that causes persons to experience forgiveness and a need to act justly. Jesus lived the will of God in towns and villages, and in the city of Jerusalem where his public ministry was conducted. He proclaimed God's reign understood by him to be a referential reality from which to judge the movement of justice in society.

Early biblical traditions record the importance of the city. The term "city" is mentioned approximately 1,760 times in the Scriptures, while 119 cities are specifically named.[3] We read that after Cain slew his brother he fled to a foreign land. Cain settled in a new land where he founded the first city.[4] The Israelite account bears witness to the perception of the city as a context that personifies human achievement.

Urbanization is positively remembered for the development of significant aspects of advancing culture—art, technology, and animal husbandry (Genesis 4:17-22). Humanity's destructive side is represented by the story of Lamech who creates the first war song in the city (Genesis 4:23-24); yet, human achievement in the urban context is not condemned by God.[5]

We read of Abraham who dwelt in the Babylonian city of Ur and the Mesopotamian city of Haran, which he left under God's guidance and promise. Scripture tells of the wandering descendants of Abraham who made temporary dwellings in or near urban areas. Cities are born of Isaac's wells, Bethel was located and named out of Jacob's dream vision, and Joseph became part of the political structure of Egypt managing the needs of its cities.[6] The empire-management role played by Joseph was particularly beneficial for some of the ancestors of Israel who entered Egypt during a time of drought and famine in Palestine (Genesis 12-50). Israel's captivity and eventual liberation in Egypt are remembered in the biblical journal to have occurred following the time of Joseph (Exodus 1:8).

The people of Israel are associated with cities right through the final occupation of Canaan, which the Scripture frames as the fulfillment of God's promise to Abraham. Israel came to control the Canaanite cities through a process of slow infiltration and by virtue of the revolt of indigenous elements of the urban populations who sought to break with the dominant feudal system entrenched throughout Canaan. The people in revolt sought to establish a more egalitarian and antihierarchical society. The religion of Israel was born out of the process of liberating struggle centralized in the urban reality of the Canaanite city-states. Yahweh chose the side of the marginal groups in the city composed by a diverse urban underclass or rejects of the dominant order.[7]

God clearly appears in history taking the side of the poor and exploited. God acts against human injustice. David's military activities created liberated zones in Canaan which extended Israelite control of the cities within these areas. The Jebusite city of Jerusalem is at the root of the "royal Zion theology" (see especially Psalm 132). David dominated the symbols and activities of religion by moving the ark of the covenant into Jerusalem, establishing a priesthood, and transforming Jerusalem into the royal city of God.[8] Jerusalem was to be a religious, cultural, economic, and social center planned to meet God's vision of community and shalom; however, with the rise of the urban monarchy, egalitarian ideals were abandoned and an oppressive hierarchical social order was introduced to rule over the whole society from the city.[9]

Prophetic literature addressed life in the city. Prophetic criticism is directed toward the city as a social institution where the privileged class who enjoyed the protection of the king increased its wealth at the expense of the urban and rural poor. A succession of prophets came not only from the marginal classes, but from cities as well. The biblical story records that Amos came from the town of Tekoa (Amos 1:1) located just a short distance south of Jerusalem. Hosea is thought to have been a city dweller; Isaiah and Zephaniah were from Jerusalem; Micah emerged out of the city of Moresheth (Micah 1:1); Jeremiah arose out of the priestly city of Anatoth (Jeremiah 1:1).[10] The prophet Ezekiel was converted during the exile to an urban perspective that included conceiving detailed plans for the reconstruction of the temple and Jerusalem (Ezekiel 40-48).

These prophets spoke out of a deep commitment to the covenant obligations engaging in the radical criticism of the corruption of the urban upper classes and the idolatrous practices typical of rural places of worship.[11] Urban corruption was rooted in the turning away from God and the obligations of the covenant (Hosea 8:14; Amos 6:8; Jeremiah 21:8; Isaiah 2:12-15). Prophetic condemnation was never intended as a message of "urban renewal."[12] Instead, the prophets envisaged a day of radical discontinuity with the system of iniquity that produced situations of oppressed-suffering for marginal humanity. Only a process of radical discontinuity could transform the city into the instrument of shalom for which God had called it into being.

Radical discontinuity came in the form of the Babylonian Captivity. The vision of a restored Jerusalem emerged from the anguished cry of a people in exile. Restoration would be announced as a sign of God's return (Isaiah 40:9). The vision of Isaiah for a restored Jerusalem directs attention toward a messianic age defined by the building of a new social order where the victims of the old oppressive system will know God's promise of fullness in life (Isaiah 65:19-22).[13] The inner city poor know the meaning of such an envisaged new order for human life together. Justice for the poor means the end of hunger, oppression, exploitation, and unnecessary death. Isaiah speaks to the experience of the poor in the ghettos and barrios.

> Behold, I will create
>  new heavens and a new earth.
> The former things will not be remembered,
>  nor will they come to mind.
> But be glad and rejoice forever
>  in what I create,

> for I will create Jerusalem to be a delight
> and its people a joy.
> I will rejoice over Jerusalem
> and take delight in my people;
> the sound of weeping and of crying
> will be heard in it no more.
> Never again will there be in it
> an infant who lives but a few days,
> or an old [person] who does not live out [the] years;
> [the one] who dies at a hundred
> will be thought a mere youth;
> [the one] who fails to reach a hundred
> will be considered accursed.
> They will build houses and dwell in them;
> they will plant vineyards and eat their fruit.
> No longer will they build houses and others live in them,
> or plant and others eat.
> For as the days of a tree,
> so will be the days of my people. (Isaiah 65:17-22, NIV)

The prophets insist that justice done to the least members of the community is a basic requirement of relationship to God. The very process that unites God to humanity is the commitment to establish life together based on the memory of a liberator God who commands that right relationship among all people take precedence over selfish interest. Isaiah makes plain that God is weary with the sound of weeping and crying in the city where the ruling forces exact the life of the poor to make them wealthy. The luxury of society has for too long been produced at the cost of the life of the working poor who build houses for others. God promises a new life together beginning with the transformation of the city where power in society is concentrated.

Jesus comes from a part of the world rejected by the Jerusalem establishment—Galilee. The region had a diverse population partly stemming from having undergone Assyrian, Babylonian, Persian, Macedonian, Egyptian, and Syrian penetration since the mid-eighth century B.C.E.[14] Jesus experienced a globalized world in Galilee, which was nothing less than a commercial crossroads where Phoenicians, Syrians, Arabs, Greeks, Orientals, and Jews were in contact.[15] Jesus of Nazareth from Galilee stood within the prophetic tradition (Matthew 16:14; Mark 8:27-33; John 4:19; 6:14; 7:40; 9:17). He identified himself as a prophet of the Jewish people at the outset of his ministry and was called a prophet by the people (Matthew 21:11). As such, he

45

questioned the system of established authority and confronted unjust earthly power.

Within the global and culturally diverse context of Galilee, Jesus directed his ministry toward those persons rejected by organized religion and neglected by society. The oppressive dimensions of globalization were represented in Jesus' day by the Roman occupation of Palestine and the Temple's legitimation of that presence; yet, the Galilean carpenter who walked with society's outcasts proceeds from the countryside toward Jerusalem, instructing the people along the way about their own oppression and turning away from God, directing attention to the kingdom of God at hand (Luke 4:18-19; 6:20-25; 12:15-21).[16]

Jerusalem was the nerve center of society. That city symbolized the concentration of economic, political, religious, and military domination for all the public. Jesus confronted power in the holy city of God at the center of Jewish identity because the oppression of the people flowed out of the institutions of Jerusalem to the detriment of society. The Temple was at the center of Jesus' confrontation with power; indeed, the Gospels focus attention on Jesus' tension with the Temple (Mark 13:2; 14:58; 15:29; Matthew 26:61; 27:39, 51). What Jesus said of the Temple was even invoked at the trial of Stephen (Acts 6:14).[17] For confronting power, Jesus was accused of corrupting the nation, encouraging the refusal to pay taxes, and posing as the Messiah (Luke 23:2).

Jesus attacks the economic base of the Temple, communicating with that incursion utter discontent with the placing of that institution in the service of selfish interests. Jesus' confrontation with oppressive power in the city of Jerusalem exposed the brutalizing reality of the established society. For this reason, organized religion and the state perceived in Jesus a threat that had to be eliminated. Jesus experiences ultimate rejection in the city of Jerusalem where the establishment marked him a subversive and blasphemer, and where close friends denied their allegiance (Matthew 14:50). The cross awaited him. Death in the city claimed Jesus' life. The homicidal structures of society conjured God's name to crucify God incarnate.

Power and glory are not the identity of God on the cross; instead, weakness and total identification with the victims of history distinguish the reality of the incarnate God crucified outside the city gates. In Jesus, the word becomes flesh in all those persons who live outside the city gates, that is to say, at the periphery of urban society. Jesus dies at the margins of the urban world just like many of today's poor and oppressed in the city. I am reminded here of the letter to the Hebrews, which is really a sermon to a group of Jewish Christians about commitment to Christ. Hebrews tells us of Jesus' death outside the city gate, and portrays discipleship as a truly costly Christian experience. Christians faced cruel persecution such as physical assault, imprisonment, loss of property, and death for confessing Christ.

The letter to the Hebrews was written to a community threatened by persecution from outside, and by strife within. In its early years, the church faced several periods of persecution, and though each had its unique characteristics, the one carried out by the Emperor Nero in 64 C.E. is illustrative. That same year a great fire in Rome reduced ten of fourteen districts in the imperial city to ashes. In the aftermath of the great fire, Jewish Christians saw the birth of martyrdom. Nero required a scapegoat to suppress the rumors circulating in Rome that blamed him for the great fire. He redirected public sentiment away from himself toward the enterprise of Christian persecution. In part, Nero rebuilt Rome aided by the sacrifice of Christians. Nero's response to the crisis of the "eternal city" included housing the homeless, lessening the price of grain, initiating an enormous urban reconstruction effort, and turning the imperial police on Christians.[18]

Hence, the catacombs awaited the persecuted Christians, providing them refuge beneath the city. To be sure, God entered underside society with the Christians who fled and hid in the catacombs, fearing death before their time. Nero's gods required priests willing to manipulate religious symbols to justify human sacrifices at the service of power and possessions. Yet, God prepares a different priesthood for humanity in Jesus Christ. Jesus represents the living sacrifice who enters the world of the oppressed, the persecuted, the outcast, and the suffering. Jesus dies outside the city gate in the stench of a garbage heap at Golgotha.

State-organized human anguish is not the final word for humanity pushed into the catacombs—life's underside. It is in just such a context that the author of Hebrews reminds the followers of Christ not to be afraid: "The Lord is my helper, I will not be afraid; what can [persecutors] do to me?" (Hebrews 13:6, NRSV). Latinos know what it means to experience death outside the city gates of established society. For Central Americans it is the security police who cause terror in the form of arrest, brutal torture, and death. For Latinos in the United States, living outside the city gates means living the reality of systemic oppression in the form of racial discrimination, social invisibility,

47

family fragmentation, urban violence and drug-related deaths, poor education, health care, and housing.

Hebrews assures the reader that Jesus' death on Golgotha places him among society's rejects and outsiders. Salvation is also experienced at the margins of society. Salvation is extended to the poor and powerless. The road to God leads directly to the poor. Jesus' death outside the city gates implies that God identifies with persons who live in what seems like a fixed state of injustice. The homeless poor and Latino families who live amid the rubble in neighborhoods crowded with abandoned tenements mirror the brokenness of the God who dies at the edge of official society "in order to sanctify the people through his own blood" (Hebrews 13:12, RSV). Salvation is not just a private experience, but finds expression in the public acts of churches and individuals who enter the world and endure abuses for Christ's sake in the hope of the "city which is to come" (Hebrews 13:14).

Finally, the powerful did not expect the return of a risen Christ whose presence reveals the future of humanity as justice and liberation. The resurrected Lord of history returned to fashion a people of God out of the urban reality of Zion. The God who became poor in Jesus Christ established the church in the city of Jerusalem. Jesus was killed outside the city gate, but God raised him from the dead and placed him in the city to demonstrate the real power of the powerless to overcome structured evil (Acts 2:23-24; 3:15; 4:10; 6:30). Urban reality calls the church to a new understanding of God that begins with immersion in the daily struggle of those persons whose voices are not heard by the powerful.

The biblical record reports that the church was called into being at Pentecost in the context of a city. The urban environment was central to the growth of Christianity across the Roman empire. The language and institutions of post-resurrection Christianity reflect urban reality.[19] Christianity spread by way of the urban environment. Paul and his associates worked and met in house churches in the context of a culturally diverse urban world. His missionary work was rooted in the urban reality of the great cities of Antioch, Ephesus, Corinth, Jerusalem, and Rome. He wrote to urban communities across broad geographic areas speaking to their needs and problems. Clearly, the city surfaces as one of God's important sacred places for the divine plan of salvation.

## THE GOOD SAMARITAN: LUKE 10:25-37

The church's mission in the city is made clear in the story of the good Samaritan. This parable features a lawyer testing Jesus' new understanding about relationship in God and human community. The questioning lawyer has a personal concern: "What must *I* do to inherit eternal life?" Jesus moves the question beyond the personal dimension. For Jesus, participation in the eternity of God's kingdom requires more than conforming individual ethics to the written law. Human experience of eternal life is not a mere matter of knowing the right thing to do, but of doing the correct thing for trampled humanity. The religion of the law is rejected for a faith that practices justice. Society's privileged ones are called into solidarity with persons who are brutalized by unjust violence and separating practices.

The Latino poor know the meaning of love that seeks justice. For instance, the Puerto Rican poor have a way of making extremely limited material wealth improve the quality of community life. Latino funerals are a context for viewing the miracle of economic distribution among the poor. I remember how the drug-related death of a member of a Puerto Rican church in New York City resulted in a deep show of solidarity for an afflicted family. Hundreds of dollars were collected by poor Puerto Ricans to provide help with burial costs. Many of those who reached into their pockets lived on fixed incomes, but did not hesitate to express action-oriented love—love that seeks justice.

The Puerto Rican church of the poor may not be completely and critically aware of the justice issues; however, death in the community becomes an occasion for demonstrating love for the neighbor as an essential condition of communion with God. Funerals are also more than a time of consolation for those who lose a friend or family member. They are occasions in the Latino community to reflect deeply on personal, social, and political issues. At the funeral I attended, older Puerto Ricans discussed the wider context within the Latino community that is marked by dislocation from the urban centers of power. Young people were reminded of the reality faced by all the Puerto Rican poor who are forced to leave their native land to live in ghettos.

The meaning of eternal life looks different for persons who live in life-denying conditions. The urban poor know that the story of the good Samaritan is about humanity left assaulted and suffering on the side of the road, social norms that require structural changes, and action geared to altering the conditions of human wretchedness produced by unjust meetings between persons in society. For Latinos, blacks, Native Americans, Asians, women, and the elderly, structural inequalities such as poorer education, housing, and job opportunities have sponsored whole communities of assaulted persons left to perish on the side of the road. Jesus tells the good Samaritan story to enable followers to grasp how God's kingdom comes in the form of compassion originating in the action of a marginal member of society.

Samaritans were disdained by their Jewish brothers and sisters. Established Jewish society, of which the lawyer, the priest, and the Levite in the story are agents, judged Samaritans racially inferior and religiously heretical; yet, God's reign of love seeking justice works through a person who knows the meaning of oppression and rejection by the established order. The Samaritan knew the experience of marginalization from the inside, thus he identified with the suffering humanity met on the side of the road.[20] Latinos stop to aid their suffering brothers and sisters on the side of the road because they know what it means to be outcasts in established white society. Globalization requires identification with those left to perish on the side of the road.

The Samaritan was willing to stop and give help because behind all the barriers placed before human experience by race, culture, and ideology stands humanity's common existence in God.[21] Grace moves us to work toward the common humanization of life together, even when it means breaking with social customs. In the story of the good Samaritan, the church learns from Jesus that God's reign is breaking into the world not by way of those who operate the old order of life; rather, the victims of the patriarchal order are being filled with God's Spirit leading the way toward the creation of an entirely new world based upon a love that establishes a better life for persons brutalized each day.

Many church persons read the story of the good Samaritan by identifying with one of the characters. Sometimes persons feel justified in believing that acting compassionately toward a friend in need makes them more like the Samaritan, while turning their backs on someone who lacks makes them more like the Levite or priest. Still, there are occasions when life causes people to feel like the assaulted person on the side of the road. Sometimes the church is even more like the innkeeper waiting for payment to aid the wounded. Having good or bad feelings is not the meaning of the story. Human subjectivity contains all of the characters in the story—Levite, priest, Samaritan, innkeeper, and assaulted humanity. The church is capable of acting out of a sense of love for those crushed by the violence of injustice or of hardening itself and ignoring human need.[22]

Jesus broadly defined the neighbor for the lawyer. Our neighbor is not merely the person in the apartment next door, on the other side of a backyard fence, in the immediate surroundings of the work place, or the person that comes knocking at the church door seeking help. The neighbor is the one who showed mercy toward the victim avoided by the religious officials who feared ritual contamination. The priest may have been a high priest whose behavior toward the victim of assault was fully dictated by social rules. Lifetime disbarment from the priestly vocation was the penalty for touching a corpse. Thus, the assaulted victim who could have died in the process of receiving assistance would be avoided by a high priest.[23]

Jesus makes it clear that the neighbor is the one whose way is taken. The church is to make itself a neighbor of those left on the side of the road to die. There is a message about globalization in this parable. Clearly, globalization means that the church is to make itself a neighbor of the nation's cities, taking upon itself the suffering of Christ (1 Peter 4:12) by immersing itself in the life of the poor and exploited of society. Christians are called to the urban world of injustice by the God present in the affliction of the poor. The church is called to plunge itself into the chaos of the urban scene where the blood of our common humanity is spilled on violence-torn streets.

What did the Samaritan do? What image of faith and ministry is given here? How is mission defined in the story? Well, the Samaritan "had compassion . . . bound up his wounds, pouring on oil and wine . . . set him on his own beast and brought him to an inn . . . took care of him . . . took out two denarii [the equivalent of two days' wages for a laborer] and gave them to the innkeeper" (Luke 10:33-35, RSV). The church will change once the neighbor is defined as the one to be looked for in urban reality and life's places of despair. The church will renew itself once it touches the wounds of the risen Jesus so apparent in the rejected humanity of the city. Looking into the face of the oppressed-poor the church will learn to say, "my Lord and my God" (John 20:28).

What is the purpose of the church in a global village? The church must discern the structure of violence in an increasingly urbanized world and promote social change. The church must become a historical agent of the radical struggle for justice. Only such a commitment to God's shalom for humanity on earth will authenticate the church's moral agency in a North Atlantic world desperately in

# *Prospect Peak*

the river runs to the edge of time
carrying the mystery of ages past
in its murky water. you can see the

little town in the valley beyond
shouting distance from Prospect Peak:
life is old in that place where generations

have followed known footsteps and
carved homes out of mountainsides
while discovering the meaning of living

only found in places beside ancient rivers.
the church steeple reaches into the sky
stretching the people's desire to know the

fullness of life in the bosom of God's
redemption. you can almost hear the
eternal echo of past ringing bells that

announce the great occasions and
celebrations which poured their way
into the town's memory with such depth

of love. they know something in
these hills gently touched by the river
whose water always flows. a divine mystery

rests in the valley ready to disclose
itself to all. . . .

need of humanizing its ethical practice. Spiritual wholeness comes from going out into the world and serving God in assaulted humanity. Reality has lacked construction on the basis of truth, thus the church must speak the truth to the powerful. Jesus tells the lawyer in the parable to go out into the world and show the compassion of the Samaritan. Perhaps this means the church needs to seek new life for the city by showing justice for the victims of violence and prejudice.

## CONCLUSION

Cities are one of God's significant sacred places, not centers of human negation and rebellion. The church is called to live out the terms of its covenant with God and humanity in the urban context. This means the church is called to engage in activity aimed at the structural transformation of society in the direction of the reign of God by globalizing its concern for justice in the city. God's involvement in the life of the city and God's profound vision of liberation for the oppressed and oppressor alike direct attention toward committed and responsible Christian involvement in urban reality.

Urban theology understood in light of the concerns of globalization requires the church to move about the rural, suburban, and urban contexts healing the sick and those unable to admit suffering. It demands engaging in a process of raising persons' critical understanding of the social dimensions of systems of oppression that structure human experience each day everywhere. It leads to the centers of society—the cities—where wealth and power are monopolized to the detriment of the well-being of God's created order. Christians are required to live consciously in society discerning the root causes of human oppression and acting to remove them.

God's design for the modern church leads directly to the city where the people of God are called to name the structures that violate the life of the poor and exploited races. Genuine globalization requires the people of God to seek the immersion of the city in which they stand—not just those cities to which they travel overseas. Christians in North America do not have to travel very far in order to understand that the economy and life-style of their society is at the root of the suffering of the poor and despised racial groups at home and abroad.

Globalization is not something to celebrate in the church until the situation of the wretched humanity of the nation's barrios is truly encountered. Globalization is not about a slide show viewed in the comfort of middle-class living rooms where photographic depiction serves to domesticate oppressive reality.

Instead, authentic globalization into the next millennium means that the church in North America will seek to critically reflect on the action of God in the city. Presently, the church is being called to solidarity with the justice struggles of international humanity in the urban world. The next chapter will examine the aspects of the history of urban development in the United States in light of the themes of globalization and human diversity.

# CHAPTER THREE

# THE CITY AND GLOBALIZATION

Global reality was a central preoccupation of the North American church in the decade of the 1980s. Christian ethics was directed toward understanding global dynamics particularly in relation to the international economic order, peace issues, and human rights violations in Central America and South Africa. Conservative and progressive religious camps each struggled to impact public policy.[1] Meanwhile, seminary and denominational bookstores stocked their shelves with books produced in the context of the justice struggles of Asia, Africa, and Latin America. First world seminarians desired to learn about how the Scriptures were being lived in Third-World societies.

The vast system of social, economic, and political ties developed across the globe over the first two-thirds of the twentieth century truly changed the way persons and whole societies viewed the inhabited world. In the 1980s, the roughly 4.5 billion people that populate the earth across six continents and scores of ocean land masses were viewed not in isolation from each other, but in terms of an interconnected web.[2] This view of interconnectedness has been reproduced in the church in terms of an understanding of human existence pictured as a system of mutual dependence. The globalization of Christian perspectives in the developed world reflects this understanding of interconnectedness. Finally, the subjection of poverty and human oppression to rigorous theological analysis became the natural outgrowth of global consciousness.

The global consciousness which deeply rooted itself over the decade

# The Seminary

halls in marble and stone
reflect that cloister look
while a voice of solemn song

floats in the air dangling
like water droplets on a leaf
before one's ear. the clean-up

men sweep sounds of work in
the corridors with the yankee game
playing on the old six transistor

radio and there are things to
tell: here comes Rene pulling his bucket
living now behind walls that

make him dream of home in Guatemala.
he was a revolutionary when love and
justice were the heart of the profession

until tyranny claimed all freedom and
the people lost all love between them
making death the settlement for disagreement

or flight to America to work for gringos
in the uniform of custodians. there are
stories to tell of refugees exiled from

another time and place never to return
save in nightly dreams. within the echoing
halls there are stories waiting for a

listening ear the soothing heart that
surely cloister walls contain somewhere. . . .

of the eighties in the North American church has enabled persons to recognize that the poor, or the earth's wretched human beings, are bearing witness with their lives to the new world God has promised in Jesus Christ. Global awareness has changed the practice of faith pursued by Christians in the context of North American society. Out of a deep sense of solidarity with the millions of persons crushed each day by systems of social, economic, political, and religious wickedness, North Atlantic ethical renewal has issued forth.

For instance, Christian denominations adopted moral and economic positions supportive of Third-World liberation struggles. Mainline Protestant denominations waged fierce internal battles over the question of the investment portfolios of pension boards. Divestment in corporations doing business in South Africa was demanded by large divisions of the membership of mainline churches. Divestment was perceived as an act of solidarity with the oppressed humanity of South Africa engaged in a struggle to dismantle apartheid. Global awareness made itself known in the life of the church particularly in the pattern of public demonstrations for peace in Central America. The renewal of a church-based peace movement saw Christians joining others in public demonstrations against the invasion of Panama and in opposition to the Gulf War.

Moreover, globalization influenced North American culture's theory of illness as evidenced in the battle against AIDS. AIDS was largely perceived by Americans as a homosexual disease; however, Christians learned that AIDS is an organic illness of the body caused by a virus. Christians heard of the illness's devastation in Third-World societies where the disease was mostly passed within the heterosexual community. Subdivisions of Catholic and mainline Protestant churches marched in solidarity with AIDS sufferers to engender a global understanding of the disease in the American mind. Solidarity with AIDS sufferers signaled opposition to homophobic attitudes which found support in an inhuman theology that asserted that God was angry with homosexuals and caused them illness.

The roots of global awareness in the United States can be traced back to the process of European occupation that began in the seventeenth century. Global processes were fundamental to the creation of the North American sociocultural reality. The Western European expansion into the land of North America, along with the early arrival of Africans on the east coast and Iberians in the Southwest, would be superceded in the nineteenth and twentieth centuries by Northern, Southern, and Eastern European settlement. Approaching the close of this century, newcomers to North America have been primarily persons from Asia, Africa, the Middle East, and Latin America.[3]

A global society was created in the United States over the course of five centuries. Native Americans were joined on the North American continent by scores of persons from all over the world to create a "nation of nations." The established, primarily white society's self-identity was challenged by the constant flow of newcomers who came with distinct cultural systems. However, Native Americans, African Americans, Asians, and Latinos experienced another "nation of nations" in white society. These ethnic groups have maintained distinct cultural identities from which to question the racist ethos and marginalizing practices often encountered in white society.[4]

Clearly, the encounter between the people of the Old and New Worlds came in the form of a cruel and brutal culture clash. The conquest and colonization of North America by Europeans resulted in the inhuman displacement of Native Americans from the land; the enslavement of Native Americans and Africans; and finally, appropriation of the Southwest territory from its Mexican base in the nineteenth century.[5] Nevertheless, as early as the seventeenth century globalization took the form of viewing the entire North American continent as a sanctuary from the political and religious persecutions underway in European society.

Sanctuary was given to black humanity by some churches in the States that joined the Underground Railroad after the passage of the Fugitive Slave Act (1850). The Act made it illegal to harbor or assist slaves seeking freedom. In the 1980s, this historical tradition was revived in the form of the new Underground Railroad—the Sanctuary Movement. The Sanctuary Movement provided safe haven to Central American refugees and empowered them with a historical platform from which to demand an end to U.S.-supported wars in Nicaragua, El Salvador, and Guatemala.[6] Global perceptions inspired the Sanctuary Movement, recalling a tradition of radical solidarity with the oppressed already woven into the fabric of life in the "new world" as early as the settlement of Santa Fe (1610) and Plymouth Colony (1620).

In the 1980s, globalization was raised like a banner by scores of persons who traveled overseas to immerse themselves in the struggles of the world's poor. Christians were excited about their contact with the faith communities in the Third World, where liberation theology and the base Christian communities were reconstructing the purpose of the church. Meanwhile, the urban context in the United States, where the poor and oppressed majority largely live, did not become a place of immersion or ecclesial renewal. Such an awareness would have caused the North American church to invite the global poor within their national borders into Christian community. Christian practice of solidarity truly transforms the church, and change is frightening!

Cities all across the country mirror the world's population, affording actual renewing possibilities for the church. Encounters with other cultural and racial communities in the urban context heightens awareness of social, structural, and historical dynamics that otherwise are mostly hidden. For North Americans to develop an authentic liberation theology and a church renewal movement equivalent to that already underway in Third-World Christian society, they must immerse themselves in urban life. Jesus weeps with the poor in the city, providing comfort to them in their struggle to radically transform the mutilating social order. Let us look at certain aspects of the development of urban society in America in light of its global themes.

## A BRIEF SKETCH OF THE EVOLUTION OF URBAN AMERICA

The so-called "new world" was inhabited in part by urban indigenous people. For instance, hundreds of years before Iberians arrived in what is today Central and South America, extensive trade was carried out in largely urban-organized Native American societies. Prehistorians have determined that complex urban societies existed in Central and South America.[7] In North America, Native Americans had already constructed cities hundreds of years before European contact. Archaeological evidence indicates that both the tribes of the Mississippi Valley and the Great Lakes Region lived in cities centuries before they experienced occupation of their land by Westerners.

Cahokia is the largest prehistoric earth-mound complex in the midwestern United States.[8] Mound Builders on the North American continent began their work in 850 c.e. Over one hundred mounds were built on the midwestern plains. Mounds were used as burial, residence, and ceremonial sites. The Cahokia Indians did not build the mounds, although these great earthworks are named after them. Nevertheless, a city numbering some thirty-five thousand inhabitants known by the name of "Cahokia" was constructed in the Mississippi Valley. The Huron of the Great Lakes region built a smaller city in which some four thousand to six thousand persons lived.[9] Urban life on North American soil begins with Native Americans—the original

# *The Block*

greying tenements called home
by old women sitting on the
front steps in silence, men

dreaming of change, and children
who learn in street play the meaning
of survival, raise their heads high

above the blacktop Cross town road.
the evenings guide neighborhood eyes
to the street light on the corner where

pause the cars of those who work in
the city but live out of town in another
world. when night envelopes the city on

the tenement steps conversation turns
to the light of imagination that slowly
constructs visions of alternative tomorrows.

sometimes mothers' heads appear at
windows calling to the sounds of voices
below the names of children requested

home. the block, that place named home,
declares all that has been lived by us.

people of the land.[10] The Spanish would later construct the first European cities on the North American continent.

For the most part, white Europeans who occupied the land between the late sixteenth and eighteenth centuries came into the new world with a largely urban orientation. Europeans transplanted their cultural views of relationship to the land, people, and all nature to the new world as well. They defined land by the terms of ownership. Western legal institutions adapted to the colonial context provided the system needed for juridically categorizing social and material relations. Private property and commerce became the foundation of life in the new world. The anthropological premise of these twin categories was the will to power and domination. Members of Euro-American society were enthralled by the promise of economic progress in the colonial order, especially given that social status in the "new world" was not marked by birth. Social status was associated with acquired wealth in the upper ranks of society.

The Southwestern cities constructed by Spanish colonizers were carefully planned according to the specifications of the Laws of the Indies (1583). Moreover, the Dutch and English urban centers of the eastern part of the continent were also carefully planned in the seats of colonial power in Europe.[11] Urban society in colonial North America was nothing less than a cautiously planned enterprise that reflected the deep connection between European metropolises and colonial reality. Largely, colonial cities surfaced on the new world landscape as the product of trade, defense, administrative, and religious needs. Urban space was a context for promoting rapid social evolution and augmented contact between diverse human groups.

Spaniards invaded the new world well over one hundred years before the English arrived on the shores of the Atlantic coast. In 1521, Mexico was conquered by the Spanish. Subsequently, blacks and Native Americans were the fuel used for some three centuries by Spain to produce wealth in colonial and metropolis European society. The process of Spanish colonization in North America began in the mid-sixteenth century with the founding of the city of St. Augustine in 1565. From this first European city in what is now the United States, the Spanish pushed westward toward Georgia and Alabama.[12]

Global processes brought a European world into direct encounter with Native America in the colonial period. To be sure, the Spanish took possession of the land, sought to "Christianize" Native Americans and practiced intermarriage. Spanish northward expansion was undertaken from Mexico (New Spain) over the seventeenth and eighteenth centuries. By the end of the first decade of the 1800s, the empire of New Spain extended from Utah to Central America. Cultural institutions such as language, religion, economics, and political assemblies fashioned a new and linked social reality in the colonial empire.[13]

Settlements were organized by Spanish friars in the Southwest territory of North America first explored by such adventurers as Fray Marcos, Alvar Nunez Cabeza de Baca, Francisco Vazquez de Coronado and Hernando Soto. Missions contributed to the Spanish settlement process in the Southwest supporting the development of cities. Cities such as San Francisco, Los Angeles, San Diego, San Antonio, El Paso, Tucson, Santa Fe, and many others in the Southwest originated under the Spanish.[14] As debate about "English only" flares, let us remember that Spanish culture almost decided the future of what is now the United States, and it continues to be part of the cultural and demographic fabric of North America.

Nonetheless, Mexico achieved independence from Spain in 1821. On the eve of independence Mexico was bankrupt, lacked internal unity, and was weakly tied to its northern frontier society. Meanwhile, Anglo-America was intent on westward expansion. Texas was to become a part of the Anglo-American world. Anglo-Americans were convinced that Texas was part of the Louisiana Purchase (1803).[15] Mexico had allowed Anglo settlers into Texas on condition that they submit to Mexican law and custom; however, they repeatedly opposed the agreement. Finally, Anglo and Mexican conflict in the northern frontier issued forth in the Texas Revolt (1836) and the Mexican-American War (1845-1848).[16]

The nineteenth century was a period of expansion for the United States. Between 1800 and 1860 the new Anglo-American nation pushed its western boundaries beyond the Mississippi River acquiring Louisiana, Florida, Texas, and Oregon. The Southwest territory was received from Mexico following the signing of the Treaty of Guadalupe Hidalgo (1848).[17] Cities were evolving industrial economies which meant that the factories displaced the small shop and home as centers of production. The United States now increased its territorial holdings by over two and a half times. Clearly, the nation was propelled by a sense of "manifest destiny," a world view rooted in the Puritan ethic, and a sense of mission to establish the "city of God" on earth.

Following the signing of the Treaty of Guadalupe Hidalgo, Mexico surrendered California, Arizona, New Mexico, and the territories currently termed Colorado, Kansas, Nevada, Oklahoma, Utah, and Wyoming to the United States. The mid-nineteenth century dispossession of Mexicans from their land resulted in steering Mexican cities toward the Anglo-American system of organization and cultural meaning. Anglo-American hegemony in the Southwest was hardly positive. In the mid-1800s, Mexicans were being lynched by whites in cities such as Brownsville and San Francisco. At the same time, Methodist circuit riders preached new birth motivated by the spirit of the Second Great Awakening.

The Methodist church historian, Frederick A. Norwood, argues that the spread of Methodism into the Southwest territory was encouraged by the Texan Revolution (1836), the Mexican-American War (1844-1848) and the discovery of gold.[18] However, the motivation for moving westward should have been the overwhelming desire to stand with Mexicans who were being brutalized by an often racially motivated, as well as rapacious, Anglo occupation of their land. Fortunately, some Anglo-Americans chose to globalize their humanitarian ethics in just such a fashion. Thoreau was one such person who opposed United States imperialist expansionism.

## URBANIZATION AND HUMAN DIVERSITY

The first Europeans to "successfully" colonize and nation-build in what is now the United States were the English. In the Euro-American colonial period (1600-1776), five port cities dominated life in the new world: New York, Philadelphia, Boston, Newport, and Charleston.[19] Colonial cities were characterized by racial, cultural, religious, and class divergence.[20] The search for opportunity and religious freedom impelled some forty million Europeans such as the Scots, Irish, Scotch-Irish, Dutch, Germans, French Huguenots, and Swedes, to come to North America in the colonial period. Jews, Catholics, blacks, and Native Americans were scattered about the colonial port cities as well.[21]

Primary resources were shipped in and out of the colonial world through the port cities. Industrialization was not the source of urban growth in the early colonial period. American urban society evolved in relation to commerce given that the colonies were linked to European centers of power through the marketplace. Cities in colonial times were essentially merchant. Moreover, the interests of the local population were subordinated to those of the European community. Meanwhile, the people of the colonial cities had to organize to build streets, improve social services, construct hygienic systems in the interests of public health, and discover more ways to meet the needs of urban society's experience of growing stress and expanding inequalities.

Many colonists arriving from Europe or migrating between cities in North America entered each context of interaction with hierarchical notions concerning human social status. For these white colonists God had ordained an unequal social structure for human experience. The view of a providentially ordered urban reality implied persons adapted to the growing social disparity shaping human experience in the city. Still, black and Native American humanity present in the cities reminded whites that other sociohistoric and cultural realities were also defining urban space. Black and Native American humanity challenged the view that the social structure was asymmetrically foreordained.[22]

At least four social groups constituted the social structure of the colonial urban environment.[23] Males tended to dominate the world of occupationally structured statuses. First, at the very top of the social hierarchy were moneyed businessmen, importers, wholesalers, investors, and, less frequently, clergymen. Local social and economic life as well as government leadership was dominated by merchants and wealthy members of colonial society. Colonial cities lacked developed legal and banking institutions; hence, wealthy merchants controlled financial and legal affairs. New world elites in North America made their wealth by engaging in local and overseas trade, moneylending and real estate ventures.[24]

The second group was none other than a rising and diverse middle class made up of artisans, shoemakers, hatters, bakers, blacksmiths, potters, butchers, carpenters, and innkeepers who provided the goods and services that kept the colonial economy running. Social solidarity often existed between wealthy merchants and the middle classes.[25] Third, persons with little or no property such as unskilled laborers, mariners, and craftsmen formed another layer of urban colonial society.[26] Working-class families lived in crowded conditions at subsistence wages. Female family members could often get work as domestics to meet middle- and upper-class needs.[27] These three layers of the city largely constituted the "white society" of the colonial world.

"Whiteness" facilitated social and easy geographical mobility within the largely English majority cities. Thus, people of color would emerge as society's permanent working poor class. The fourth group of the urban colonial city forming a permanent marginal class were both Native Americans and free and enslaved blacks. To be sure, after the revolution the free black population increased significantly in towns such as Richmond, Baltimore, Boston, New York, Philadelphia, Cincinnati, Charleston, New Orleans, and Mobile.[28] In time, ex-slaves would migrate to urban centers where greater concentrations of free blacks and emerging black institutions assured systems of support.

The clergy were respected figures who managed to exercise considerable influence in private and public affairs in the urban environment. Urban ministry mostly consisted of defining and legitimating the social order; however, growing religious pluralism represented by competing Protestant sects soon challenged the hegemony of any single organized religious body. Moreover, the Great Awakening (1730s and 1740s), which was rooted in the colonial cities, further give rise to persons that challenged established theological tradition. Preachers like George Whitefield and Jonathan Edwards attracted scores of urbanites and small town dwellers eroding the once assured hegemony of the educated clergy—Puritan or Anglican—that almost exclusively defined the meaning of the colonial social order.[29]

## THE EMERGENCE OF NATIONAL URBAN SOCIETY

Cities were also becoming centers of resistance where the authority of the European state and church was questioned. The revolt against "British Pharaoh" was partly planned in the cities where human resources for organizing revolution were concentrated. People met in homes, coffeehouses, printing shops, and bars to debate and plan their revolt. Women were able to play a critical role in the revolutionary process, in part owing to their observance of the boycotts of imported goods and participation in social protest against colonial rule. Moreover, they kept the social economy alive during the absence of men away fighting the revolutionary war.[30]

The Spanish and the French supported the American revolt against British colonial rule. On January 1, 1777, at the age of twenty-nine, Bernardo de Galvez (after whom Galveston is named) was appointed governor of Louisiana by the king of Spain, Charles III. By June, 1779, Spain was at war with England. Galvez, who captured numerous English forts, received reinforcement troops from Cuba, Mexico, Puerto Rico, Haiti, Venezuela, and the Dominican Republic. His army grew to a force of seven thousand men—mostly black, Native American, and racially mixed persons.[31] Galvez defeated the English in Louisiana, Alabama, and Florida six years before the American Constitutional Convention (1787), and supported the American Revolution with his own troups. New Orleans served as a city of refuge for persons who fought against the English.[32] Spain's support for the

American Revolution contributed greatly to the success of the American colonists' independence movement. Thus, on the North American continent, global politics and cross-cultural contact helped the processes of nation building.

Urbanization entails the process of the growing influence of the city over society. Urbanization accelerated following the American Revolution by which the United States was formed. For instance, the influence of urbanites at the Constitutional Convention held in Philadelphia in May 1787 was quite strong. Despite the fact that a mere 5 percent of the national population was living in urban environments at the time of the convention, well over half of the fifty-five constitutional delegates were either urbanites or city-oriented. State ratification of the constitution was favored particularly by city dwellers.[33]

The American Union produced a constitution to run the affairs of the new nation. Urban commercial interests were advantageously incorporated into the new constitution in the form of regulative stipulations and economic centralization geared to limiting individual states from establishing independent trade and monetary policy.[34] Meanwhile, church bodies breaking from the "mother" churches of Europe underwent similar processes of reconstitution.[35] Indeed, it was in this period that the Methodists officially broke their ties with England and became a national church.

Already American society was becoming largely urbanized by the middle of the nineteenth century. Moreover, between the mid-nineteenth and the early twentieth century, American cities received new immigrants such as the Chinese, Japanese, Jews, Southern and Eastern Europeans, Italians, Greeks, Armenians, Portuguese, Magyars, Syrians, and Latin Americans. The Slavs were represented by Russians, Ukrainians, Slovaks, Slovenes, Poles, Croatians, Serbs, and Bulgarians.[36] Clearly, the presence of whites, blacks, native Latinos, Native Americans, and foreigners in cities laid the foundation for a rich globalized urban environment.

Interestingly, negative and positive images of the city began appearing in mid-nineteenth-century literature. The social historian, Andrew Lees, reports that religious antiurban writings were represented by such Protestant ministers as John Todd, who wrote negatively of Philadelphia, and Reverend Amory D. Mayo, who articulated antiurban attitudes of New York City life.[37] In addition, Ralph Waldo Emerson, James Fenimore Cooper, Herman Melville, Edgar Allan Poe, and Nathaniel Hawthorne all expressed negative sentiment about the city. Emerson, Cooper, and Hawthorne later saw the city more positively in works published in the 1850s and early 1860s.[38] Yet, the poet and journalist, Walt Whitman, took a pro-urban stance holding that restless humanity discovered its own depth in the city.[39]

White society largely accepted the new immigrants from Italy, Russia, Hungary, Romania, and other European nations.[40] These groups could assimilate over time into the established communities. However, racist attitudes shaped relations with Asians, Latinos, Native Americans, Arabs, and blacks. Chinese and Japanese immigrants who came to America in the mid-nineteenth and early-twentieth century were greeted by anti-Asian sentiment and suffered extreme oppression and discrimination in housing, jobs, and education. Laws were passed by white society in attempts to disenfranchise Asians, such as 1) the Chinese Exclusion Act of 1882, intended to keep the Chinese out of America, and 2) the Oriental Exclusion Act of 1924, intended to exclude all Asians.[41] After Pearl Harbor was bombed on December 7, 1941, Japanese Americans were placed in so-called relocation centers.

## NATIONAL URBAN SOCIETY

In the nineteenth century, developing transportation technology such as the railroads facilitated the process of industrial and economic growth and created a linked national urban system. The countryside had managed to avoid the influence of urban culture exercised over society since the American Revolution; however, the railroad system ended rural independence by making the countryside the supplier of the urban world's raw materials.[42] Urban mass transit permitted the upper and middle classes to escape the city to settle in outlying areas.[43] Urban central business areas were practically displaced by regional businesses meeting commuter needs along public transportation routes. Neighborhoods flourished in the outlying areas. The flight to the suburbs by the city's prospering members left much of the inner city to the poor who had fewer resources or social forces for combating the growing urban problems of poverty, poor housing, and inadequate public health care.[44]

Persons were attracted to cities inspired by dreams of economic opportunity; yet, Latinos, Asians, Native Americans, and blacks continually encountered hostility in white society and were often marginalized in the urban economy. The United States ended the century with the colonization of Puerto Rico in 1898. The occupation of Puerto Rico signaled the beginning of the so-called "American century" in which the United States would surface as a world power.[45] Obviously, historical processes such as migration and U.S. expansionism contributed to the populations that made American cities global villages where cultural, racial, religious, and class diversity was evident.

Urban growth continued over the first four decades of the twentieth century. Urbanization typified the nation's social process. Millions of people poured into the city in the early 1920s to take advantage of the potential economic opportunity that the growing industrial economy might offer. Interestingly, the movement of Native Americans to cities had been underway since the General Allotment Act of 1887 which assigned Native American reservation lands to whites. In Brooklyn, New York, a Mohawk Indian settlement came into existence. The Mohawks migrated to the city to work building bridges and skyscrapers.[46]

Parts of the United States not located in the Southwest were "latinoized" with Puerto Ricans and Cubans taking up residence in New York and Florida. Mexicans could be found living in Chicago and Detroit. Blacks left the south and streamed into the nation's cities. Already in 1919 racial riots occurred across the nation's urban landscape, indicative of increasing conditions of race polarization.[47] Meanwhile, Mexicans were denied the right to vote, organize in unions, or share public facilities. School segregation in Texas and California for Mexicans also quickened.[48]

Interestingly, racial segregation in public schools in the United States has been viewed as a largely black and white issue. However, legal precedent for the famed *Brown* v. *the Board of Education* case (1954), which ended legislated racial segregation in the schools, was established by challenges to segregation suffered by Latinos in schools in Texas and California. The racial separation of Chicanos in schools was ruled unconstitutional in 1946 in the ruling by Judge McCormick who heard the *Mendez* v. *Westminster School District* case of Southern California, and in 1948 under Judge Ben H. Rice, Jr. in Texas who heard the *Delgado* v. *Bastrop Independent School District* case. White and black societies largely view school desegregation as their issue, but Latino legal cases paved the way for school desegregation.[49]

Little urban development occurred from the period of the Great Depression (1929) until the end of the Second World War (1945). Cities did, however, enter a new relational stage with the federal government in the 1930s under the New Deal administration of Franklin D. Roosevelt. New Deal federal agencies were established such as the Emergency Relief Administration (FERA) that provided state and local municipalities with budgets to meet the needs of the destitute; Civil Works Administration (CWA) that enabled temporary work for the poor (1933-34); the Public Works Administration (PWA) through which projects like the Triborough bridge in New York City were made possible; the Work Progress Administration (WPA) under whose auspices public parks, buildings, and hundreds of miles of highways were built. In an eight-year period, WPA employed some 8.5 million people and contributed to urban revitalization.[50]

Suburban development was bolstered as well in part by the congressional creation of the Home Owner Loan Corporation (HOLC) in 1933 and the Federal Housing Administration (FHA) in 1934.[51] Public housing erupted on the urban scene toward the end of the 1930s and into the 1940s, sparked by the creation of the United States Housing Authority (USHA) following the passage in 1937 of the Wagner-Steagal Act. Senator Wagner of New York gained the support of Roosevelt who pushed Congress into adopting the bill. The Wagner-Steagal Act was especially helpful to the black population and persons at the lower third of the economic ladder. Moreover, the housing problems of the ghetto were not in any way erased, although housing stress was reduced.[52]

The suburban development boom issued forth in the years following the Second World War and well into the 1970s. Inner cities had become increasingly nonwhite in composition given the "white flight" to the suburbs facilitated by systems of mass transportation, automobiles, the creation of highways, the movement of businesses to outlying areas and housing developers who responded to postwar residential shortages by catering to the home ownership dream of members of the middle class.[53] But the suburbs developed as a largely white phenomenon. This pattern of exclusive evolution was fueled by institutional racism in the form of FHA initial refusal to back suburban loans to persons of color and Jews.[54]

Post-World War II America saw the development of the civil rights movement by which black humanity engaged in collective behavior opposed to racial discrimination and economic inequality. The modern civil rights movement of the 1950s and 1960s originated largely in Southern cities where economic boycotts and nonviolent protest marches were strategies for confronting white society. The year-long Montgomery bus boycott was sparked by longtime racial equality activist, Rosa Parks. She refused to give her bus seat to a white man on December 1, 1955. Because she broke local segregation law, arrest followed.[55] Dr. Martin Luther King, Jr., who related the gospel to the struggle for justice until his assassination in 1968, led the year-long boycott.[56]

## URBAN DISCORD AND FISCAL CRISIS

The civil rights movement peaked in the mid-1960s following the passage by Congress of the Civil Rights Act (1964) and the Voting Rights Act (1965). Despite these legislative achievements, there was rioting on city streets. In the summers between 1965 and 1968 approximately seventy-five riots occurred in cities across the nation.[57] Riots during this period were often sparked by perceived police brutality; however, violence took the form of arson and looting of mostly white-owned retail establishments located in the ghettos and barrios. Black and Latino humanity rioted to protest white society's systematic marginalization of persons of color in the social order. Mostly, blacks and Latinos were injured or killed by police, not in clashes with whites.

In the early 1960s, American society discovered the nation's inner-city poor. President Kennedy read Michael Harrington's *The Other America* (1962), which painted a grim picture of a prosperous society indifferent to the "invisible land" of the poor. In 1963, Kennedy announced interest in launching an antipoverty legislative program; however, it was Lyndon Johnson who would make the War on Poverty a distinctive feature of his administration. Johnson's War on Poverty was intended to end unemployment and poverty in America and establish the so-called "Great Society." The War on Poverty programs of the Johnson administration were supposed to empower the poor to transform their lives.

In 1964, Congress passed the Economic Opportunity Act (OEO), that established the Office of Economic Opportunity. Antipoverty programs administered by OEO included the Job Corps, Head Start, Vista, Legal Aid, and the Community Action Program. In 1966, a Model Cities component was started as an effort to combat social problems in housing, education, health, welfare, and employment. Antipoverty programs were conceived to make the poor partners in the execution of national social policy. Mostly, the poor were not empowered and dismal urban social and physical conditions continued despite the billions of dollars spent. Thus, the War on Poverty simply served to win Democratic Party support in the nation's ghettos.[58]

Cities entered the decade of the 1970s experiencing fiscal crisis.[59] During this era of financial stress, the urban economy lost its tax base to the suburb, Sunbelt, and overseas competition. New York City lost six hundred thousand jobs between 1969 and 1976 alone. Had the city not lost these jobs, tax revenue would have amounted to $1.5 billion dollars and the fiscal crisis could have been averted.[60] These structural changes in cities forced a decline in public revenue, private income, and employment. Consequently, city services such as mass transit, public works, social welfare, the police, fire, and sanitation departments all declined.

Urban decline and abandonment were symbolized by the South Bronx. For instance, tenements on Home Street where I grew up were left to decline by owners who decided that their buildings were not profitable. Local factories moved away resulting in a major increase in unemployment for residents. My family was hit hard by the fiscal crisis in the city. We observed how the absence of capital to repair old tenements resulted in the abandonment of tenements by landlords. High rates of chronic unemployment forced a dramatic increase in poverty and social stress. Over time the South Bronx acquired the look of a war-bombed city. Extreme poverty and death were the marks of the wretched conditions of the South Bronx.

In the early 1970s, the South Bronx experienced the abandonment of twenty to thirty thousand housing units yearly.[61] Buildings were burned regularly, reaching a level of approximately thirty-four a day toward the middle of the decade.[62] Unscrupulous landlords would sometimes ask neighborhood junkies to set fire to their tenements in order to collect insurance. Several junkie friends of mine would charge a small fee of two hundred dollars to set fire to a building. I recollect that on occasion angry residents or neighborhood kids would also set fire to the abandoned tenements in futile protests against poor housing conditions and declining city services.

Black and Latino politicians rose to power at this time and were left with the enormous task of reconstructing the cities. Black mayors surfaced in Gary, Cleveland, Newark, Atlanta, New Orleans, Chicago, Detroit, Philadelphia, Birmingham, Richmond, Los Angeles, and Washington, D.C. Latino politicians came to power in such cities as Miami, San Antonio, and New York.[63] At once, American cities were also receiving immigrants and refugees from Asia and Latin America.[64] Thousands came from Cambodia, Laos, and Vietnam fleeing the war (1959–1975). Economic recession also resulted in white reaction to the growing numbers of foreigners "taking jobs."

Nevertheless, cities continued to express themselves as multicultural realities where people could become true "global citizens." By the end of the 1970s, the city was back in fashion as urban real estate developers and municipalities lured wealthier groups such as the new "young urban professionals" (*yuppies*) into run-down neighborhoods. Gentrification meant a new class of young professionals was returning to the city and moving into remodeled buildings and historic townhouses. The poor were being forced out of their homes and communities when rents were going up and wages were not. Those who were able "suburbanized" during this period, moving to cities just outside large urban areas. Countless more joined the ranks of the homeless.

## THE CITY IN THE 1980s

The 1980s opened with Ronald Reagan announcing to the world that America was back. America "came back" declaring war on the poor at home and overseas. Billions of dollars were funneled into Central America during the Reagan administration years. For instance, the military and police forces more than doubled in countries such as El Salvador and Guatemala. North American cities acquired many refugees from these countries. The nation's capital experienced enormous growth in its Salvadoran population. Over three-fourths of Latinos in Washington, D.C. are Salvadoran refugees. Salvadorans currently constitute the second largest racial-ethnic group in the nation's capital.

America was back reestablishing hegemony in Central and South America and in international affairs. The Nicaraguan Bay of Corinto was mined by the United States, the embargo on the sale of arms to the government of South Africa was lifted, and Grenada was invaded by American troops. Meanwhile, the problems of urban poverty, inequality, and decline were not priority issues for the federal government in the Reagan era. Instead, billions of dollars were cut from domestic spending in the areas of education, housing, health care, and income maintenance programs. The church itself did not make the situation of the national poor a priority issue of Christian ethics.

Cities and states suffered severe cuts in federal aid such as 37 percent of the $35.2 billion budget cuts in fiscal year 1982.[65] Between 1982 and 1984, the Reagan administration cut spending to domestic social service programs in the amount of $140 billion. Income maintenance

# 14th Street

an exhausted Saturday afternoon
holds in its fleeing arms latino
smiles themselves first shaped on

islands in the ocean and villages
in Central America. from all across
the city they have gathered in this

market place where a listening ear
can hear latino nations speak through
the memory of refugees and the independence

dreams of Boricuas. they gather
to cradle each other in history for a few
moments and drive away their invisibility

in America. stories are shared about
when the land in El Salvador will grow
food for the people instead of export, of

undocumented Nefatali who made his way
to New York from the Dominican Republic
arrested last week in a factory raid,

of the pregnant junkie mother Leonor
who gave birth to twins infected with
AIDS, and the little Methodist church in the

barrio with closed doors all week. beside
a merchandise bin two women speak of how
the children are having difficulty at school,

roam the streets, and are left alone. they
remind each other how that was the road
which led Hector into a grave at age 10

from a drug overdose. here the world of
latino struggle encounters a language
of hope deeply carved in the hearts of

exiles from another land and those who
are born strangers in this place called

the United States of America. . . .

programs serving the needs of the poor absorbed over half of the budget cuts.[66] The logic underwriting the Reagan administration's national urban policy prescribed movement away from federal grant programs toward creating a "free enterprise" economic environment that supposedly would stimulate private-sector investment to finance jobs and urban renewal.[67]

Race and class polarization increased during this time in the nation's cities. Urban racial discord was symbolized by the death of a young black man in Howard Beach at the hands of angry whites. Blacks clashed with Korean immigrants running small businesses in inner city neighborhoods.[68] In New York City's Thompkins Square Park a summer riot occurred toward the end of the decade over housing issues and the fight against gentrification. The Lower East Side was being gentrified by young professionals who were placing pressure on the local police to "clean" the park of a growing homeless population. Local activists arranged a protest focused on housing for the homeless living in the park. The police excited a riot by cruelly beating homeless activists and innocent observers of the protest.

Extremes of urban inequality could be discerned in city neighborhoods where the so-called "yuppies" busily restored newly acquired brownstones just blocks from urban parks and public spaces that had become domiciles to homeless families. The homeless were not social dropouts; instead, they were men, women, and children excluded from the social system, but whose labor was exploited for a meager minimum wage. By the end of the decade, the United States Mayors Conference began to study the impact of Reaganomics on the urban environment. The United States Conference of City Human Services Officials and the Mayors Conference focused national attention on urban inequality understood as the process of the rich getting richer at the expense of the poor.[69]

The U.S. Conference of Mayors discovered that over the decade of the 1980s hunger, homelessness, and poverty were increasing in the nation's cities.[70] The antipoor ideology institutionalized in the form of Reaganomics had created a marginal class in urban society never experienced before in the nation's history. New York City alone had a homeless population of some sixty thousand persons by the middle of the decade and many more were underhoused. Homelessness was not primarily the result of social pathologies such as mental disorders, drug abuse, or character weaknesses. Homelessness was related to the housing-for-profit system understood as the process whereby city-owned properties were sold to private developers for luxury apartments. Housing for the poor declined as apartments in choice city neighborhoods went "condo."

By the close of the 1980s homelessness, hunger, and poverty were on the increase in American cities. In 1988, twenty-seven cities surveyed by the U.S. Mayors Conference revealed that requests for emergency food assistance and shelter were going up; however, the resources to meet the needs of the growing ranks of the poor were declining. Persons experienced mounting urban stress as a result of chronic unemployment, underemployment, decreasing monies for public assistance, and lack of affordable housing. Americans discovered that many of the nation's homeless were working poor families surviving on minimum wage and forced to live in shantytowns, city shelters, out of their cars, or in abandoned buildings in the inner city.

Many of the cries of the poor came from families with female-headed households, which by the mid-1980s numbered some 3.6 million. Black and Latino children were especially hard-hit with 46 percent of the black children and 41 percent of Latino children living in poverty. Now, just nine years from the start of the twenty-first century, some 33 million people live in poverty in the United States, although researchers believe the numbers are higher if those not counted—such as "illegal aliens"—are added. Over 13 million children in the United States live in extreme poverty. Some 1 million teen-age women get pregnant each year, while 18 percent of all infants born in the United States' city hospitals are delivered addicted to crack, alcohol, or some other hard drug.[71]

Social inequality is partly explained by an economic structure that permits the richest 20 percent of American families to receive 44 percent of the national family income and the poorest 20 percent only 4.6 percent.[72] The poor know greater health problems, drug and alcohol abuse, inadequate education, lack of adequate social services, and inferior living conditions. Some children of poor families contract diseases associated with the so-called "Third World" such as whooping cough and tuberculosis. Sadly, the ranks of the poor will grow larger in the 1990s as the economy continues to contract, jobs are exported overseas to cheap labor markets, and the national deficit grows. Social struggle in the future will be increasingly revenue-driven as cities enter a new age of fiscal crisis.

Interestingly, in the 1980s cities experienced a dramatic increase in crack-cocaine abuse among young people. Crack reality in the city was in part generated by the Reagan administration's dirty war in Central America. Key figures in the administration concerned with financing a

Contra victory in Nicaragua engaged in covert operations and cocaine-based fund raising for the so-called "freedom fighters" operation. Drug smuggling resulted in a 1,000 percent increase in cocaine traffic by the close of the decade. Drugs and drug-related violence in the urban world is a sign of social illness. This illness points to deep social despair arising from the breakdown of community and social institutions capable of engendering hope.

American society holds up luxurious dreams of making it economically. However, for the poor and oppressed who suffer the disfigurement caused by living in conditions of wretchedness, the dream is actually a survival nightmare. Sadly, inner-city youths are increasingly participating in urban informal economies in the form of crack dealing. Drug dealing presents a way of making it in a society that measures human worth by money. Meanwhile, social ethical institutions like the church hardly address the despairing humanity of the welfare hotels, condemned buildings, and junkie-tormented street corners. Thinking globally has hardly led to local action on behalf of suffering humanity in the city.

Observation of economic dynamics in the city reveals that drug cartels, corporate food chains, real estate firms, and state lottery ticket sales benefit from the millions of dollars spent by local inner-city populations. Money spent by the inner-city poor represents a form of export capital in that it does not get reinvested in the local community; instead, it leaves the barrios and ghettos to benefit those who prefer to maintain systems of wealth production which to them are deemed nonoppressive. Because the city is a global reality where all humanity meets, the church must engage in a ministry of accompaniment in the totality of the dynamic reality of the urban world.

## CONCLUSION

The church's concern with internationalizing its theological perspective on social ethical issues points to the city as a context for globalization. This chapter explored the way cities in the United States developed from the colonial period to the present as dynamic multicultural, multilinguistic, and multiracial settings. Clearly, the city concentrates the flesh and blood of humanity from all sides of the globe into a single geographic space bringing into sharp focus the future of society. From the mid-nineteenth century it was clear that the future of the United States was the city defined as a complex world in

# Lamentations

stoops the block hangout
for city streets where Crack 45
and Miller High Life are served on

the altar of sacrificed lives. young
latinos pursuing highs raise shouts of
praise to Gods most like their own

strungout pain. Angel, Lelo, Rudy,
Rosa all names colored by inheritance
and changed by the American dream

Lelo the sailor,
Rudy the junkie-thief,
Angel the drunken mailman
Rosa the pimp's old lady

how fortunate for us to be "spiks"
in the land of opportunity, how great the
march of liberty in 1898, how lucky that

Time Magazine gave us a place in history
by claiming a full decade to be the day
of the "hispanics" in a world that never

turns its head our way to see the road
ahead lined with signs reading everything
remains the same the same the same. . . .

which the movement of larger national and international dynamic forces could be charted.

To be sure, humanity has come to cities in the United States from all parts of the world partly stemming from shifts in the social structure of their society related to global politics and economics. For instance, the movement of refugees from Africa, Asia, Central America, and Eastern Europe to cities in the United States is clear evidence of the global connection that exists between societies linked by an international political economy. Nevertheless, United States' expansionist interest in the nineteenth century resulted in the occupation of Mexican territory in the Southwest and the incorporation of Mexican cities into an Anglo-defined, white society.

Surely, urban space particularly affords the church an opportunity to engage humanity from all parts of the world on its own soil. Moreover, the large presence of black, Latino, Native American, Arab, and Asian humanity in the city also permits the white church to face a counter voice that challenges established white society's reading of history. In the urban context Christians will discover sharp contrasts between the affluent and the growing ranks of the poor to whom the church is sent by God. Globalization means nothing less than honestly encountering the multicultural reality that underwrites urban history in the United States. Hence, the church has the rather enormous task of seeking immersion in the reality of cities. The global poor were making their way to North American cities, but few in the church paused to take notice of them.

# CHAPTER FOUR

# GLOBALIZATION:

*Encountering Some City Voices*

## THE JEWISH HOLOCAUST

North American Christians are in the process of developing a more global perspective on their reality. The idea of globalization caught the imagination of the local church in the early 1980s. I reason that globalization's historic roots are in the period of the Second World War. The systematic annihilation of Jews in Hitler's Nazi Germany made Christians confront a terrifying global political reality. The Jewish Holocaust buried the North Atlantic sentiment of Christian triumphalism. Jewish suffering and death required the church to critically reflect on its efforts to oppose Hitler's order of state-sponsored terror.

Clearly, one sector of the Christian community legitimated the systematic annihilation of Jews. Jesus' message of justice was not applied by this subdivision of the church to Jewish humanity. Another body of Christians did not shrink from the challenge of reformulating faith tradition in light of the profound requirements of God's justice for all humanity. The stench of burned flesh billowing in the world atmosphere from the Nazi ovens could no longer be evaded or denied. Globalization in the church is rooted in the terrorizing encounter with the reality of the Jewish Holocaust; moreover, that horrifying reality opened North Atlantic Christians to the disquietude of the oppressed at home and the Third World poor.[1]

# *The Doorway*

in the shadow of doorways
the night spent and light rising
above sleeping tenements among heaps

of gathered clothing sorted now for street
sales they sit. motionless at the first sign
of day they listen to the inner voice of a

past life as laughter creates a home in
street places. dressed in colors thrown
together they ask sleepy workers for coffee

change some will use for daily wine.
each day these homeless are moved to the
edge of the world castigated

by certain anonymity—a nameless fate.
listen, the first church bells ring in the distance
and the street people grasp memory filled bags

for the long march of day to travel
till night when rest will again
demand another doorway

for street sleep. . . .

## THE BLACK CHURCH

The black struggle for liberation was one dimension of the global disquietude that overtook the post-World War II world. White society confronted globalization in the United States in the black struggle for racial and economic justice. Persons connected to such organizations as the Southern Christian Leadership Conference, the National Conference of Black Churchmen, the Interreligious Foundation for Community Organization and black alliances in white ecclesial structures developed a prophetic protest model for social change between the 1950s and 1960s.[2] At the same time, the civil rights movement became a major constitutive element in the development of Black Liberation Theology. The black church, speaking from the particularity of race, demanded the moral reorganization of white society in light of God's Word concerning the equality of all persons. Black Christians—and those who stood with them—risked their lives promoting social justice in light of their commitment to the God of the oppressed.

James Cone published *Black Theology and Black Power* in 1969. Cone's book articulated the theological meaning of black power for white society. White society saw the gospel of Jesus of Nazareth become reinterpreted from the perspective of the black struggle for justice in a racist social order. White society listened closely to the activities and discourse of the black struggle, although not typically in solidarity. Nevertheless, the memory of the Holocaust of the Second World War assured that some white Christians were more open to the voices of the oppressed around them.[3] White churches had to face the negation of their racial interpretation of Christianity by the black church. Globalization now signified that God was not a white racist.

Armed with the gospel of Jesus Christ—a savior who knows the meaning of oppressed suffering—black Christianity challenged the racist ethos of white society. White Christianity's tradition of segregated worship was challenged by the gospel interpreted through the experience of black humanity. Black Christians preserved in their crucified flesh the truly subversive memory of Jesus who died on the cross—accused as a blasphemer and political rebel—for the cause of justice and humanized existence. Black Christians denounced the missional practice of the established white church that theologically justified hereditary slavery for three centuries and supported segregation in the South.[4] The black church placed religious life at the service of political action against pervasive racism and economic injustice in white society.

# *El Garaje*

clumps of metal bent to
fit the space adorned another
morning of work at the garage.

oil blackened hands hold
a freedom never known by the
world's condemned in the labor

performed. just now a wino
stops before the building next door
to snatch up crumbs left leaning

on the tenement and trampled on
the sidewalk but the hunger surrenders
to the power of a needed drink

searched for in the brown paper bag.
soon, the garage doors swing open to
receive another poverty convicted car

into its womb while a neighborhood
priest walking by looks in at the
heaps of rusted steel the smiling

face of the repairman wondering
about life as a mechanic.

What does globalization mean in terms of the encounter with black humanity? First, it entails immersion in the city where the existence of a black marginal class, ignored by the white church, continues to grow daily at historically unprecedented rates. The growth of the black oppressed and poor is rooted in systemic realities that remain largely unexamined by the church. Second, a mostly racist ideology contaminated white society and its religious sentiments at the cost of black lives. For years God has been conceived by many North Americans as a member of the white world. Many members of the white community largely repressed the confession of the Word made flesh in a member of an oppressed class and race.[5] Globalization means that white Christians must confront their racism through dialogue with the black church.

White and black Christian persons need to confront the distinct "otherness" of their traditions and experiences, offering interpretations that direct their ethical and political energies toward God's unifying reign. Globalization for white society means adopting a new perspective on Christian tradition that interprets God's relation to humanity from the situation of oppressed blacks. Third, globalization understood as the encounter with a unique other exposes the fact that racial and economic conditions of oppression represent situations of injustice and death. White Christianity will only be transformed by way of this type of authentic meeting with black Christian experience. Theology must not be segregated from the reality of racial diversity in the context of real human unity under God.

Conclusively, the black church has played a central role in the liberative struggle of black humanity in the United States and overseas. The black struggle for freedom was viewed by the oppressed overseas as a symbol of hope for all oppressed and exploited humanity. The black church restored dignity to men, women, and children devalued by racism in white society; it supported the development of financial and educational institutions in the black community; and provided a critique of the racist morality of white society.[6] The black church demands that all Christians direct their energy toward eradicating racial and economic oppression. The black church revealed how religious forms and symbols can be powerful vehicles for socially and politically organizing communities to promote their own values and historical agenda.

The global promise of the black church tradition of North America is: Christianity everywhere can and must appropriate the faith tradition in nonracist terms. Black Christianity's mission perspective for white society includes the image of a reconstructed white society moving in the direction of the vision of humanity made plain by God in Jesus of Nazareth.[7] Globalization means listening to the profound insight of black Christians who can tell the universal church about the racist ideology that permeates much of the North Atlantic church's faith tradition and discourse. Surely, church communities transformed by their encounter with black humanity will opt to do everything possible to eradicate racism from their world.

Yet, the reformulation of the racial ethic of white society alone has proven insufficient for combating the continuing growth of poverty and oppressed-suffering that strikes at black humanity and persons of color at home and overseas. Globalization as the mutual encounter of human diversity in a world longing for freedom means that the black church will have to direct part of its gaze toward the global and local poor's struggle for liberation.[8] A greater share in the structure of inequality, which is produced by the political economy of the United States, negates the pursuit of such alternatives as integration into the material social process of white society.[9]

A deeper vision of Christianity's meaning for the transformation of life together needs to be reflected by the black faith community situated in the North Atlantic world. Embracing God means seeking to establish a new social order that judges its fidelity by the justice done to the poor and oppressed classes. God's kingdom for human reality means living into an alternative embodiment of social reality based on relationships of justice and equality at every level of existence—economic, racial, political, social, cultural, and spiritual. These missional priorities are not alien to the black church tradition; however, the time for their renewal has arrived. The reality of a globally interconnected world requires missional renewal. The black church needs to recapture its self-understanding as a religion of the poor concerned with the transformation of the social order, rather than fostering class mobility within it.

The black church can enlarge its practice of faith by listening to the Latino church at home and abroad. Latino theology, shaped by liberation theology, promotes a class analysis framework that advocates a nonclassist appropriation of the faith tradition. Barrio theology demands the economic reconstruction of the North Atlantic order so that the oppressed and poor can experience the kingdom as a time when "they shall not build for others to live in, or plant for others to eat" (Isaiah 65:22, RSV).[10] Human suffering caused by the widening gap between the haves and have-nots—especially visible in cities around the world—demands that the black church wed its powerful history of struggle to the vision of a humanity freed from economic systems that structure poverty and oppression into life. Failure to oppose economies of death means negating the very essence of black Christianity, which is rooted in the struggle against the slave economy.

Hence, the black church must press on toward seeking an alliance with the struggles of Latinos and the oppressed at home and in the Third World. A broadened vision of solidarity into the next century means unfolding a clearer understanding of the causes of global suffering and impoverishment issuing forth from the political economy of the developed world. Moreover, the black church, called by the reality of nonwhite distressed communities at home and abroad, needs to link faith to the quest for a just global order. This vision of a new global order is fundamentally intolerant of systems of structured evil emanating from social modes of production that result in daily crucifixion for most persons. Globalization understood in terms of mutual theological interpretation and dialogue between oppressed communities means engaging in a process of collectively reclaiming histories of struggle to aid in the construction of a better world.

## FEMINIST AND WOMANIST STRUGGLES

Since the early 1960s, Christian women have engaged in a radical critique of the largely androcentric or male-centered perspective of North Atlantic theology. Patriarchal culture largely considered the historical experience of women insignificant. Androcentric theology denied the humanity of women by devaluing their presence and importance in the Christian tradition. Males defined their issues as having ultimate significance for the church and in critical theological discourse. The linguistic framework of church tradition was mostly male-centered for centuries. Male pronouns and images of God communicated religious experience to the exclusion of the female members of human society.

Because the naming of reality provides the conceptual framework for human social relationships, feminist theology centered much attention on language, raising questions about male definitions of actuality. Feminist theological reconstruction of the tradition contextualized language about God in the reality of a cultural milieu devaluing women.[11] Christian feminists have taught us that it is possible to engage in a nonsexist appropriation of the faith tradition. This nonsexist appropriation of the Christian tradition requires persons to understand the meaning and language of power in a patriarchally constructed world.

Women placed the patriarchal paradigm of the canonical tradition under radical critique. Feminist scholars who focused attention on the patriarchal structure of Christianity have recovered the feminine aspects of the tradition. The feminist rereading of the tradition demonstrates how the male-bias undermines the requirements of the gospel's message of justice and wholeness for all humanity. The Scriptures use male and female metaphors in narrative descriptions of God. In part, feminist theology requires Christians to understand God's "dual sexuality" by supplanting male God-talk and male-centered visions of humankind that are exclusive of women and promote their domination and oppression.[12]

Women have a long way to go before the cultural pattern of patriarchal society is dismantled. However, in the present century, women improved their status as cultural actors in society sufficient to make significant contributions toward changing their peripheral role in politics, economics, and religion. The emergence of feminist theology is a product of the same history that saw women begin to struggle and tell "her-story." Feminists have enabled the church to discover women's particular way of embodying the image of God. Moreover, feminist theological perspectives have broadened the meaning of sociocultural terms such as equality and liberation. Males are now listening closely to women narrating their experience of God, the mother. Feminist thinkers have promoted a growing awareness of women's faith wisdom nurtured in the deep silence of time.

Feminist theology represents a political discourse of empowerment. Feminists read the Bible in light of the experience of women who, having been mostly dislocated from the economic and political structures of society, seek to change organized power. Doing theology from the perspective of women transforms Christian perceptions of power and domination. Feminist theology underscores the importance of examining the relationship between a dominant patriarchal social order and its negative impact on the humanity of women. Feminists have used culture theory to emphasize the historical character and plasticity of gender. Gender roles in society are not biologically determined, but are culturally assigned.[13] Thus, sex-specific social roles can be redefined in light of new cultural understandings of the place of women and men in society.

At another level, feminist scholars made the public aware of the extent to which poverty has become a largely female problem. Between the 1960s and 1970s, during the heyday of the nation's civil rights and peace movements, poverty began to be feminized. By the mid-seventies, two-thirds of America's poor persons above the age of sixteen were women.[14] The sociologist Diana Pearce coined the phrase, "the feminization of poverty," often noting that the majority of poor Americans were women.[15] Poverty's feminization is influenced by occupational segregation, the lack of adequate public benefits and services to support women in the labor market, the failure of equalization policies like affirmative action and pay legislation, and social realities such as divorce and teen-age motherhood.[16]

Women comprise over three-fifths of the nation's labor force; however, they are often forced by the cultured expectations of motherhood to work part-time and use the remaining time to parent. Part-time work has fewer benefits and openings for job advancement. Overall, women are mostly segregated in low-paying and low-status jobs in the service and retail industries. Divorce and teen-age motherhood combine to work detrimentally against women's economic status in society. Often, divorced mothers and teen-age mothers must care for children and cannot enter the labor market. Professional women still greatly experience the male-female wage gap. For black and Latina women, job market inequities and lack of social support systems are made worse by racism.[17]

## WOMANIST-MUJERISTA THEOLOGY

The inherent limitations of feminist hermeneutics issued forth in the late 1980s in the voices of black and Latina thinkers.[18] The corrective discourse of women of color consisted of diverting theological and Christian ethical attention to the specificity of race and ethnicity as theological categories of social and political struggle. White feminists could do theology without entering into solidarity with the poor and oppressed; however, womanist and mujerista theologians made the preferential option for the oppressed and poor central to their theology. For women of color, the pursuit of questions of ultimate theological meaning results from a profound ethical commitment to the daily lives of women oppressed by poverty in a racist society.

One of my most memorable personal encounters with the corrective

# *Must Mean Something*

the corner is wet today
where the buildings once stood
rain pours over the dusty lots.

the people roaming the length
of street, condemned just like
the buildings, have been sent away

to live at the edges of yet another
world for waiting, mourning, and
remembering to lift their fallen

heads: the corner is wet with
the sounds of children that no
longer play, a young sister that

never walks alone, an old man with
rum for a walking stick, a grandmother
that sits in her living room chair

each day forgetting memories
while staring at a clock that
doesn't work and listening for

the postman's footsteps on the
other side of her apartment door.
a gentle rain falls, a quiet drizzle

we think must mean something.

discourse of women of color came one summer in Peru. The maternal face of God met me in the faces of the oppressed and poor women of Peruvian society. Peru has been in a period of economic decline since the mid-1970s. The government of Peru is incapable of creating conditions of life of benefit to the population. The nation's more than $20 billion national debt increases human wretchedness daily. Shantytowns stretch across the city of Lima, where public services like water and electricity are not readily available across the urban landscape. Existence is precarious in a nation where the average monthly income is approximately forty-five dollars.

I was told by the people of the shantytowns that poverty is death and injustice. The human cost of poverty appears on the faces of children, who contract diseases like tuberculosis from poor nutrition and lack of medicine. Urban reality in the city of Lima confronts Christians with the cry of a people whose very flesh and blood incarnates a social and global structure of existence that serves the interests of persons who never smell the stench of shantytown garbage heaps. Yet, in the middle of the crisis of reality in Peruvian society, women surface as cultural actors who collectively defend the life of the poor from the forces of hunger, impoverishment, dehumanization, injustice, and death.

The maternal face of God was most clearly visible on an afternoon in El Comedor del Corazón de Jesus Cristo ("Community Kitchen of the Heart of Jesus Christ"). In Peru, the women have organized to respond to the crisis of their society by collectivizing the family food problem. The food shortages are no longer a private family concern; instead, the problem of scarcity and malnourishment has been transformed into a social issue. The Comedores give new meaning to the petition in the Lord's Prayer concerning daily bread. Women are living the words "Give us this day our daily bread." They have organized work into the necessary force that transforms reality into human sustaining bread.

Comedores (Community Kitchens) are signs of God's bread in the form of social solidarity and community activism. The institution of the Comedores enables Peruvian women to engage in a tradition of mutual help with roots in the pre-Columbian period. Native American communities organized life around systems of mutual aid or reciprocity long before the Spanish invasion and settlement. Women are using a cultural tradition of mutual aid that is centuries-old as a resource for sustaining modern Peruvian society at the most elemental levels. Women run the Community Kitchens helping to meet the subsistence needs of a people living between poverty and death.

Comedores are the maternal face of God. The women running El

Comedor del Corazón de Jesus Cristo understand their role in society as that of defending the life and dignity of the poor. God's hands and feet busily work preparing daily meals in the Community Kitchen for hungry men, women, and children who daily enter Peru's world of informal economy to earn small amounts of money to maintain their lives. The formal economy of Peru hardly benefits the masses of poor people who have organized informal systems of exchange to produce and reproduce life. Hence, grass-roots organizations like Comedores are important units of production in people's lives.

What do women do in the Community Kitchen? First, Community Kitchens provide a space for women to break out of the isolation of domestic life. These grass-roots institutions are a context for the redefinition of women in society. Second, women gather in the Comedores to engage in critical reflection, raising questions ranging from the sexual division of labor to the international debt's impact on local communities. Third, grass-roots organizations like the Comedores are centers for women's social and political participation in society. God speaks in the voices of the women of Peru's popular organizations, telling those who would listen that God opts for the poor and hungry.

I was told repeatedly by the women of Peru that God opts for the people. The grass-roots organizations in Peru impressed upon me this faith perspective. In a time of utter crisis, the women of the grass-roots organizations represent the stabilizing force of human existence. Since 1975 official Peruvian society, imaged by the government, has offered the poor of Peru growing conditions of misery. Yet, women in Peru have organized into communities of empowerment defending the human rights of the poor from structured oppression. Organizing to change the harsh conditions of social reality most certainly means challenging the distribution of power in Peruvian society. Globalization in the context of Peru means recognizing that women are empowered by God to bring life from the chaotic conditions of death caused by maldistributed power and resources.

For centuries, women have struggled collectively to give shape to a reality that is more just than that of patriarchal society and its systems of domination. God the mother has been present in their actions from the beginning of time. For me, the motherhood of God shone on the faces and in the lives of Peruvian women, whose actions bore prophetic witness to the reign of God at hand. When the masculine and feminine sides of God enter history, the Word becomes real flesh. God is loving, just, liberating, powerful, and revealed for appearing in history as women affirming life over death. Surely, God's maternal face in the biblical record is evidenced in the acts of women.

The Hebrew Scriptures speak of prophetic women such as Huldah (2 Kings 22:14), Deborah (Judges 4:4), Miriam (Exodus 15:20), Judith, Esther, Ruth, Tamar, Anna, and the unnamed prophetess in Isaiah (8:3). God made use of the lives of these women to impact the economic, political, and cultural structures of society.[19] In the New Testament, the Matthean genealogy places Tamar, Rahab, Ruth, and Bathsheba in prominent roles. In Luke-Acts, women exercise important roles in the community of Jesus—Elizabeth (Luke 1:36); Anna the prophetess (Luke 2:36); women who supported Jesus, including Mary Magdalene, Joanna, and Susanna (Luke 18:1-8); Tabitha of Joppa (Acts 9:36); Lydia (Acts 16:14, 40); Mary and Rhoda (Acts 21:8, 9).[20]

Womanists remind us that Jesus' mother was no ordinary woman. For instance, Luke attributes the Magnificat to Mary, although the words are taken from the prayer of Hannah (1 Samuel 2:1-10). Mary of the Magnificat is portrayed as a radical visionary, a revolutionary, and the mother of a revolutionary. Mary's words in a country like El Salvador or Guatemala would mark her as a subversive and an enemy of the status quo. Mary, who comes from the poor, is deeply committed to the justice struggles of the *anawin* (the destitute). Mary reminds me so much of the women in the Comedores. In the Matthean and Lukan resurrection accounts, women were the first witnesses to the empty tomb. Angels chose these first witnesses to explain the resurrection of Jesus Christ.

In the Pauline epistles, the status of women is best displayed by Galatians 3:28 and Romans 16:1-16. Some attribute to Paul texts written from an extreme antifemale perspective. However, those narratives signifying the subordination of women are largely found in the so-called "Deutero-Pauline" writings such as Colossians, Ephesians, 1 and 2 Timothy, and Titus. Paul's own stance recognizes the leadership of women and the need to dissolve sex-specific distinctions in the community of Jesus.[21] Clearly, globalization means that the church recognizes that the prominence given to women in the biblical tradition links God's struggle for human liberation with feminine reality.

## GIFTS FROM NATIVE AMERICA

Globalization in the Americas means encountering Native American reality as well.[22] For the most part, white Europeans brutally encountered Native Americans on the soil of the "Americas," taking possession of the land, resources, and labor of the inhabitants of the new world. Today, the system of economic, political, social, cultural, and religious imperialism imposed following the conquest continues to exist in the oppressive poverty of Native Americans in the Western hemisphere. In North America, over half of all Native Americans live in cities. Their urbanization resulted from the Land Allotment Act of 1887.[23] Overall, life conditions are so abominable for Native Americans that the term "fourth world" is used to name their reality of extreme poverty and oppression.[24]

The idea of Manifest Destiny drove Western Christians into the new world fueling their expansionist impulse and zeal for missionizing non-Christians. Whites believed that God had chosen them to Christianize and civilize the so-called "heathen" people of the new world. White Christianity interpreted the mission of the church from the perspective of the powerful. The missionary's project focused on converting "racially and culturally inferior" Native Americans into the image of Western humanity; however, even this image was qualified by the conquerors' need to subhumanize, enslave, and exploit the indigenous peoples to create the luxurious wealth of colonial and metropolitan societies.

Christopher Columbus named the diverse Native American nations encountered in the Western hemisphere "indios" (Indians).[25] White society's renaming of the native cultures implied the negation of the richly diverse and complex nature of native societies found across the Americas. Nineteenth-century Euro-American society in the United States denied Native Americans the capacity for social evolution and cultural creativity. Early American anthropologists argued that indigenous societies were holdovers from earlier evolutionary stages. The great mound-builder controversy focused energy upon whether or not the mounds of the Ohio and Mississippi Valley were erected by "indians" or another lost race of people—perhaps, the lost tribes of Israel! The mound-builder controversy was really about the denial of cultural productivity to Native Americans who were thought inferior to whites.[26]

White society promoted a process of cultural genocide against indigenous peoples. White religion played a major role in justifying to a large extent the political, social, and economic hegemony of the West. The spiritual understanding of native peoples was devalued and judged by the white expropriator to be devoid of authentic communication from God.[27] Many white European Christians could not accept the possibility that Native American culture possessed spiritual truths originating outside of a Western Christian reality. Native American truth claims were considered mere primitivism. Most whites believed that the metaphysical truths of Native American cultures could not contain anything of universal value or revelatory significance.

For the most part, mission history reflects that Christians of white society sought Native American spiritual and cultural conquest as a precondition for entry into Christian life. Native Americans were expected to adopt the habits and dress of white culture as a mark of authentic conversion. This logic of identity alteration defined the mission enterprise of white Christianity, contributing to the justification of social and cultural policies that resulted in near extinction and death in fourth-world existence. Presently, Native Americans are inviting the North Atlantic world to God's table a second time. Globalization in this context means listening to the voice of Jesus who is the crucified Indian of the Americas.

Christian globalization during the period of expansion and brutal conquest in the new world required the Westernization of encountered cultures, belief, patterned behavior, and theological understanding of divine disclosure. Today, Christians are realizing that the self-revelation of God is communicated to other cultures in their particularity. The universality of God's reconciling act in Jesus Christ meets persons in their cultural context. A growing awareness of God's created and diverse cultural plans has enabled white Christianity to admit that divine truth exists in nonwhite humanity communicated in the specific cultural codes that relate ultimate meaning.[28]

White Christians have had difficulty surrendering to non-North Atlantic peoples the authority of their truth claims. They largely overlooked the fact that all truth claims are rooted in particular cultural contexts. God's word is always incarnate in a particular place, time, history, people, and culture. Jesus preached the kingdom of God to Jews in Palestine. The primitive church struggled with the question of the extension of Jesus' mission to the Gentiles.[29] The deculturation of the missionized was never a demand of the gospel; rather, the gospel speaks of the inculturation of divine actuality and bears witness to the Word becoming flesh. Christian mission implies living the truth of the gospel in the reality of persons' distinct cultural universe and sociohistoric struggles.

## GLOBALIZATION AS SPIRITUAL ENCOUNTER

Globalization as the encounter with Native America means learning about indigenous spirituality. In the United States some four hundred Native American nations exist, each with a distinct way of life.[30] Indigenous cultures in the Americas root their spiritual experience in the earth or specific sacred lands. Western humanity's relationship to the land has presumed the need to dominate, control, and exploit the natural world. Problems with the planetary ecosystem are a result of this human will to dominate and exploit in the service of monetary profits. The world view of Western industrialized market societies separate human beings from nature. Western soteriology posits human salvation outside of the natural order in individuals and society.[31]

What can Native American spirituality contribute to Western Christianity? First, Native American spirituality shifts the starting point of Christian theology from Christology to the great mystery of the whole of God's creation. Hence, a new way to think about God-in-Christ reconciling the world is to listen first to the integrity of creation that groans for liberation (Romans 8). The rapaciousness of market-oriented modes of production and their threat to the ecosystem demands reflection on the vitality of creation. Native Americans believe that the church's concerns about peace and justice should be pursued in light of an authentic creation theology that recognizes the interrelationship and sacredness of all things.[32]

The Native American's creation-centered sense of reality can deepen the spirituality of the West, fostering a true sense of liberation. Globalization understood as the encounter with Native American Christianity means approaching the faith tradition with a new set of eyes. This new lens of Christian spirituality is the concern for the totality of creation. Western Christianity's theology will acquire a very different hermeneutical orientation, once it develops a spirituality that understands the natural order from the perspective of universal salvation.[33] Moreover, Western Christian ethics will not only focus on issues related to the person in society, but will also develop eco-ethical reflections to guide the church's liberating praxis in the world.

Western spirituality must discover a holistic sense of the sacred by globalizing its faith perspective by listening carefully to the wisdom born of the soil in the memories, stories, and struggles of Native Americans. Indigenous peoples perceive the goodness of nature: God's incarnational presence in creation, and humanity's sin against

God by the daily violation of the natural world and the human life within it. Only the God who enters human history from the margins could grant such a deep awareness to humanity. Native America is God's kingdom at hand. Thus, indigenous Christianity gives the universal faith tradition a new sense of the blessedness and interrelationship of the cosmos. God is all in all.

Second, entering into dialogue with Native American Christians will also help the church recover a deeper sense of God's story of liberation. All Christians agree that God is known in this tradition through the descriptive narratives of the Bible that preserve the memory of a people delivered from oppression. Nevertheless, the church has forgotten to tell God's story, preferring to rationalize about the divine mystery sustaining creation. Theology is the intelligence of faith, and sharp reasoning helps the process of Christian formation; however, faith knowledge is not demonstrated by strictly producing persons capable of engaging in rational theological discourse. Christians must learn the stories of faith that speak of a God who enters human history as an act of political resistance to the few who oppress the many. Doing theology means telling the story of saving acts.

Jesus taught in parables showing how the Word becomes incarnate in life's ambiguities and struggles. Christians of first-world societies need to recover a sense of storytelling that is honest about the conflict in history. God is apprehended in the life of the oppressed, who enter history as agents of a new vision of humanity and as just stewards of the created world. Telling the story of Christian participation in the struggle of the whole created order for liberation images the pattern of narrative description found in the biblical reports about the reality of God. Native Americans demand honesty from Euro-American society about history. From Native America, North Atlantic Christians can learn that God's biography is the whole of creation moving toward justice and wholeness.

Globalization is more than a process of encounter for white Christianity with communities overseas that are radically different. Instead, it represents a movement within church life concerned with breaking down the walls of separation between diverse groups at home as well. White Christianity in the United States is called by God to discover the richness of its own context for engaging in the process of global awakening. The globalizing church in history provides people with a new reference point in their lives—God's reign incarnate in all humanity! For the globalizing church encountering Native American humanity, this means standing outside of imperialist interpretations of history that justify systems of oppression and domination.

## ARABS IN THE CITY

Yet another opportunity for breaking down walls of separation among peoples exists with Arabs in the United States. Recent events in the Persian Gulf have, however, not always shown Americans at their wisest and most conciliatory. President Bush entreated the American public's moral sense by professing a "conviction to oppose injustice" as the basis for the "just war" against Iraq. President Bush's "conviction to oppose injustice" did not prevent the sending of economic military aid to El Salvador the day before the start of the aerial bombardment of the city of Baghdad.[34] That moral stance has not guided the United States' action to decolonize Puerto Rico, deny military aid to the government of El Salvador after the murder of six Jesuits and their two employees, or oppose the long history of Israel's brutal treatment of Palestinians. But Americans did express moral outrage toward the Gulf War. On January 26, 1991, two hundred thousand persons converged in Washington, D.C. for an antiwar demonstration to oppose Bush's election of military action over sanctions and diplomacy.

The Gulf War resulted in over one hundred thousand Iraqi civilian deaths and tens of thousands of people injured. The small nation of Iraq located in the region of the Middle East known as the cradle of civilization and associated with the very genesis of biblical monotheism was bombed back to "pre-industrial" times. The new world order emerging in global history is not defined by East-West conflict. That new order was suggested in President Bush's rejection of the Soviet peace effort that had secured agreement on Iraqi withdrawal from Kuwait and restoration of the Kuwaiti government.[35] The principle of North Atlantic self-assertion underwriting the new world order is familiar in the Third World. President Bush's Gulf War served to establish United States ascendancy in the new world order as well as foreshadow the North-South conflicts to come.[36]

In June, military dress parades were staged in cities around the country to counter the Vietnam syndrome and promote social integration around the theme of the "liberation" of Kuwait and the United States' perception of the conquering democracy. Meanwhile, in liberated Kuwait scores of workers labored overtime to restore the luxury of the palace of Emir, Sheik al-Sabath. Moreover, Iraqi cities lay in ruins lacking usable water, electricity, food, and medical supplies, and civil war raged between Saddam Hussein's troops, Kurds, and Shiites.[37] North America fought an unnecessary war supported by media coverage that falsely projected Arab consensus behind Saddam

Hussein. Anti-Arab racism increased in the United States causing unnecessary suffering to Arab-Americans in such cities as Detroit and Dearborn in the form of vandalized mosques and businesses, and drive-by shootings.

North Americans are relatively unaware that Arabs have been emigrating to the industrial urban areas of the United States since the last quarter of the nineteenth century. The countries of the Arab world with representative populations in the United States are: Algeria, Bahrain, Egypt, Iraq, Jordan, Kuwait, Lebanon, Libya, Morocco, Oman, Palestine, the People's Democratic Republic of Yemen, Qatar, Saudi Arabia, Syria, Sudan, Tunisia, The United Arab Emirates, and the Yemen Arab Republic.[38] Early Arab emigrants came from Mt. Lebanon, an autonomous district in Syria prior to World War I that was administered by a Christian Ottoman official answerable to the Sublime Porte in Istanbul.[39] Although early Arab emigrants were mostly Christians from Mt. Lebanon, Syria, post-World War II Arab emigration included more Muslims.

Over twelve million Arab Christians live in the Middle East and scattered in countries around the world. Approximately one-fourth of all Arab Christians live in North and South America.[40] Arab Christianity is organized into three branches termed the Orthodox, Melkite, and Marionite. One form of Arab Christianity evolved under the tradition of Constantinople termed Byzantine Rite Christianity (East). Byzantine Christianity matured at the level of local communities given the absence of an overarching politico-religious center as found in Roman Catholicism.[41] Roman rite Christianity (West) affected the growth of Melkite and Marionite traditions. While Marionites always claimed Western identification, Orthodox Syrians who transferred allegiance to the Roman rite church in the early eighteenth century are called Melkites.[42]

Muslim Arab civilization was in ascendancy from the seventh century until the renaissance in Europe. The Islamic faith, whose name means submission to one God revealed through the prophet Muhammad, is recorded in the Quran. The holy law recorded in the Quran constitutes a formal rationality that encompasses every aspect of life for adherents of Islam. Islam is imprecisely connected to Christianity and Judaism. Muslims consider the rocky outcropping site in the center of the old city of Jerusalem a major holy place. Arab Muslims have been settling in the United States since the last quarter of the nineteenth century. Thousands are now living distributed in various parts of the United States, especially Dearborn, Detroit, Quincy, Rochester, New York, and Washington, D.C., among other cities.

Christians in North America can learn a great deal from their Muslim Arab neighbors. For instance, Islam teaches that social responsibility and communitarian values are central to their submission to the one God. These deep social values oppose the consumerist and egocentric perspectives of American culture largely reinforced by an enculturated Christianity. Nevertheless, Islamic cultures' interpretation of the role of women in society and in relation to men needs closer examination. The church can improve North American understanding of Arab culture by cultivating relationships with leaders of the Arab and Arab-American communities in the United States. Contact with such organizations as the Washington, D.C.-based American Arab Anti-Discrimination Committee, the leadership of known local Arab membership mosques or other Islamic institutions will help break negative stereotypes and foster real globalization with members of a world the West needs desperately to understand.

## CONCLUSION

Theologians agree that globalization as the mutual interpretation of culture and faith tradition constitutes a response to the inadequacy of the *theologia perennis* produced in the context of the North Atlantic world and forming the recorded history of its ecclesial tradition.[43] Classical theology and ecclesial practices supported the vested interest of the established order, and promoted the oppression of women, Amerindian, black, Asian, Arab, and Latino humanity. Hence, doing theology in the richness of God's cosmos requires the modern church to engage in a process of genuine contextualization. Globalization is the process that makes the Word flesh in the reality of other human beings.

The Jewish holocaust ends the sentiment of Christian triumphalism. Moreover, Native American Christians teach the church to develop a pro-creation theology; black humanity teaches white Christians to appropriate God in nonracist ways; women point to the importance of developing a nonsexist concept of God and theological language; Latinos promote a nonclassist seizure of the faith tradition; womanists make central the categories of race and ethnicity in their ethic of struggle; and Arab humanity is affiliated with both Christianity and Islam holding communitarian values as an ultimate concern. Globalization as contextualized Christian experience in the multicultural, multiracial, and class-diverse context of the city gives the church a new compass for understanding human diversity in history.

Globalization implies that the church is ready to discern God's presence in the contrast of cultural experience. Hence, critical reflection on the gospel in light of human diversity requires greater attention to cultural realities. The gospel is never heard outside of cultural systems of belief and behavior. The history of Christian thought from the advent of the patristic writings to the present, confirms that theology has always been contextual or culture-bound.[44] Surely, the great insight of the process of globalization is its admission that human beings devise systems of meaning through their cultures.

Finally, churches concerned about the process of globalization need to develop ways of listening to other cultural voices. We have briefly reviewed some of these voices present in the urban context. I am convinced that a way for the church to develop a greater capacity to discern God's presence in the cries for justice emanating out of diverse cultural settings in the city is to make use of the science of anthropology. Anthropology is a social science for the study of human diversity within the specificity of integrated cultural systems. The unique approach to human experience developed by anthropology can contribute to greater contextual understanding and renewal in the church. Chapter 5 will examine what I term pastoral anthropology in relation to globalization. Chapter 6 will provide a cultural immersion approach for church use.

# CHAPTER FIVE

# PASTORAL ANTHROPOLOGY

Theological anthropology has generalized about human social life and behavior by drawing primarily upon scriptural and Greco-Roman sociocultural categories.[1] However, globalization challenges the church to elaborate new understandings of human belief and behavior. Current talk about globalizing North American Christian perspectives suggests that the church intends to take cultural diversity seriously. Cultural anthropology's study of human diversity reveals that God-talk cannot be expressed monolithically because it is always culturally stationed. Theology must think in terms of human diversity. The church must learn to understand the role of culture in constructing theological reality in the context of human diversity within a single history.

Pastoral anthropology is an approach to cultural diversity aimed at helping local church communities understand how religion as a cultural institution shapes knowledge, attitudes, and behavior through its symbol and knowledge systems. Pastoral anthropology as a strategy for the study of religion presumes that culture is the context of human behavior and belief. Ultimately, the globalization perspective implied in pastoral anthropology is concerned with the "existence" and "significance" of cultural belief systems over questions of the "truth" or "falsehood" of particular religious frames of reference in culture.

Pastoral anthropology gives serious attention to theo-ethical perspectives articulated by the religion of cultural groups that have experienced the weight of unequal development over the course of global history. White society only gains significant insight into the

101

character of God revealed in Jesus when it recognizes that its cultural symboling implies epistemological limitation. Any study of the culturally constructed theologies of white and nonwhite humanity shows different perceptions on the scriptural tradition. I will not attempt to review the many cultural realities to be encountered in the city; however, after discussing the value of anthropology, the concerns of pastoral anthropology will be illustrated with specific Latino sketches.

## THE DEVELOPMENT OF ANTHROPOLOGY

The discipline of anthropology developed into a modern social science in the late nineteenth and early twentieth centuries. Anthropologists originally relied on the reports of missionaries, travelers, colonial administrators, and amateur students of culture for descriptions of alternate human experiences. Anthropology's professionalization over the first several decades of the twentieth century resulted in the establishment of the ethnographic method, or fieldwork.[2] Fieldwork involved research based on sustained immersion within a living culture. Ethnographic accounts produced by anthropologists after their fieldwork experiences focused on the rich diversity of cultural reality.

The development of the ethnographic method made notable contributions to human knowledge. First, contextualized cultural research challenged Western civilization's presumptions about universality and taken-for-granted concepts, such as the nuclear family.[3] Second, cultural orders came to be viewed as malleable systems of belief and behavior expressive of the particularity of social traditions advanced over time. Third, research based on sustained interaction with other cultural realities resulted in the placement of a profound value on human diversity. Sensitivity to the diversity of human experience implied the recognition of the plasticity of cultural phenomena which, in turn, provided a basis for North Atlantic cultural self-critique.[4]

However, the North Atlantic world's preference for uniformitarian concepts of culture assured disregard for the great complexity and diversity of humanity. Uniformitarianism is rooted in enlightenment conceptualizations of culture that portray the vast array of human cultural variability across space and time homologously. The church itself appealed to uniformitarian concepts of evangelization to interpret the meaning of catholicity in the early period of Western global expansion. Catholicity meant uniformity interpreted in light of the North Atlantic world's *orbus christianus* ideology![5] Enlightenment "anthropology" dismissed culture to posit the essence of humanity as reason, but modern anthropology again dressed humanity with culture.[6]

Culture is the central concept of anthropology; yet, no absolute definition of culture dominates the field. Anthropologists make use of cultural definitions that best illumine the particular aspects of human experience they wish to investigate. James Lett argues that three salient paradigms drive anthropological investigations: 1) cultural material- ism—an approach concerned with the question of causality and the interplay between society's material and ideological structures, 2) symbolic anthropology—the approach concerned with the significance of meaning-systems for the construction of human identity and the organization of society, and 3) structuralism—an approach that traces perceived universal structures of the mind and cognition.[7]

Human beings produce life and identity in the context of culture. What is culture? Culture is the institutionalized pattern of belief, norms, values, and behavior acquired by a member of a social group through which experience in the world is sorted and made intelligible. Culture is the life-way fashioned by human beings serving as the base for meaningful interpretations of existence. All human interaction in society is mediated by culture. More importantly, cultural domains viewed from a globalization perspective need to be understood in terms of the history of the new world that has been linked in a process of unequal development.[8] Globalizing church communities are required to locate the cultural "other" in historic contexts that elucidate the interplay of centuries of social, political, economic, and cultural dynamics.

Globalization pays particular attention to the church's articulation of the role of relations of domination in the production of social relations. Thus, theological communities concerned with the project of globalization must not dislocate culture from the material social process. Culture viewed from the perspective of history entails developing a political economic approach to the study of human diversity. Globalization implies that close attention will be given to the world-wide social process of uneven development deriving from asymmetrical power relations in history. Culture history[9] represents an anthropological approach that promises to illumine more profoundly

# *Papi of Another Shore*

he walks the Avenue coughing
the cold air and dreaming of latinoamerica,
a third family left behind, the one he'll

die beside, forgetting the son enslaved
by a Bronx street. he walks grateful to
the nation that gave him a home which he

never lived, unable to understand
why the young Latino men and women
of the country never learned to call

this home, yet not having any other.
Papi comes to the American shore to live
the merchant seaman's life expecting Port

children to give a home and call him
father while leaving them with stories
of the sea and condemned as the "hispanics"

of America. he dreams of having more
in his Latino country paradise and living
like royalty on social security perched

in a place rich with poor he can no
longer understand. . . .

for the church the relations that obtain between North Atlantic society and the world of the Southern hemisphere.

For cultural historians, human communities need to be grasped within the particularity of their respective experience, but in terms of global processes of history. Pastoral anthropology makes use of a culture history approach to locate language about God within the processes of culture in history. Pastoral anthropology seeks to understand the context of theology in light of the social, political, economic, cultural, and religious processes that shaped them. Pastoral anthropology contributes to greater contextual and historical understanding of the dynamics constituting the experiential framework of human communities: thus it serves the globalizing church's interest of transforming encounter.

## CULTURAL HISTORY: BRIEF LATINO SKETCHES

The term "Hispanic" is used to collectively refer to Spanish heritage persons in North America. It projects a unity that masks racial, ethnic, national, and cultural diversity. "Latino" is the preferred label by politically conscious members of the Spanish heritage community in North America. The term "Latino" articulates the reality of a community becoming aware of its own social, political, and economic power to make history. The collective label "Latinos" provides a conceptual framework for organizing opposition to cultural devaluation and socioeconomic oppression.

Twenty million Latinos live in the United States. Latinos can be found living in every state of the United States, although 85 percent of the U.S. Latino population is concentrated in nine states—California, Texas, New York, Florida, Illinois, New Jersey, New Mexico, Arizona, and Colorado. The three largest Latino populations in the United States in descending order are the Mexican, the Puerto Rican, and the Cuban. Central and South Americans represent another growing subdivision of the Latin American community in the United States. Latinos in the United States experience greater levels of educational disadvantage and higher rates of unemployment and poverty than the general population.[10]

North American society seldom recognizes Latino cultural diversity. White society's use of the collective label "Hispanic" operates out of a set of assumptions that suppose Latin Americans to have a common culture and socioeconomic status.[11] Persons of Latino ancestry in the

United States display different culture histories and socioeconomic realities between them. There are even Latinos in the States today with no tradition outside of the country, such as the "hispanos" of New Mexico—descendants of sixteenth-century Spanish settlers. Latin Americans in the United States have experienced different histories leading to incorporation in American society.[12]

**Mexicans:** Mexican society was rather dynamic prior to the American conquest. Independent Mexico possessed a vast portion of the "American West" such as California, Arizona, New Mexico, Texas, Nevada, Utah, and western Colorado. Sections of Wyoming, Kansas, and Oklahoma were also part of the North American continent acquired by independent Mexico following the break from Spain in 1821. Yet, Mexican frontier life was isolated, depending for communication largely on the metropolis represented by Mexico City. Conflict with the native Americans who opposed occupation of their land served to further isolate frontier society.

Cultural change in Mexico's northern frontier was already underway as early as the late 1820s when the frontier began to Americanize as a result of Anglo-American economic and demographic westward expansion.[13] Members of Mexican north frontier society already held largely ambivalent loyalties to Mexico by the time the American invading forces reached them. Foreign markets invaded Latino northern frontier society following Mexico's independence, helping to break the isolation of the past. Anglo-American military conquest and annexation of the Southwest actually finalized a process of separation that was rooted in the dynamics of Mexican society following independence from Spain in 1821.[14]

Open conflict with Anglo settlers characterized life for Mexicans between 1820 and 1848. White settlers viewed native Mexicans as trespassers in the Northwest territory. Texas was the first area of conflict between Mexicans and whites. According to Rodolfo Acuna, the roots of the conflict can be dated back to 1767, when Benjamin Franklin gave voice to American expansionism by naming Mexico and Cuba expected possessions. Thomas Jefferson also held that Texas belonged to the United States, acquired as part of the Louisiana Purchase in 1803.[15] Already in the early 1800s, the United States had established posts in the Spanish territory of Florida. In 1819, the Adams-Onis Treaty was signed, ceding Florida to the United States and causing the United States to back away from claims to Texas.[16]

The 1820s were marked by growing conflicts and attempts to

establish an independent Texas Republic. Whites objected to the Adams-Onis treaty, believing that Texas belonged to the United States and could not be turned over to Spain by the U.S. government. White sentiment for autonomy was expressed in 1819 by James Long's unsuccessful attempt to establish the Republic of Texas, and by Hayden Edwards, who took over the town of Nacogdoches (1826) and named it the Republic of Fredonia.[17] The Edwards Revolt was successfully repressed by the combined efforts of Anglo-Americans and Mexico. Aggressive U.S. foreign policy was implemented when, in 1826, the Mexicans refused John Quincy Adams' one-million-dollar offer for Texas.[18] The Texas Rebellion of 1836 finally resulted in whites declaring an independent Texas Republic.

White invasion of the Southwest accelerated in the 1840s, giving rise to the Mexican-American War (1845–1848). Mexico surrendered half its territorial holdings (a land area brimming with rich natural resources) to the United States at the conclusion of the war with the signing of the Treaty of Guadalupe-Hidalgo (1848). The treaty specified that Mexicans would be protected under the constitution of the United States. However, Mexicans were not given the protection promised them by the treaty. American conquest resulted in social, cultural, political, and legal conflict.

White society's conquest of the Southwest transformed Mexicans into a "minority" of the United States. The Mexican "minority" was recast into a segregated, racially despised, and cheap labor force.[19] Profound ideological perspectives fueled the conflictual relationships between Mexicans and whites in post-conquest reality. The historian David Weber[20] explains the origin of negative stereotypes of Mexicans, who were stylized stupid, lazy, vain, ignorant, and "scarce more than apes." Many historians have argued that negative Mexican stereotypes are the result of culture clashes between whites and Mexicans in frontier society during the twenty-five years preceding the Mexican War.[21] Weber, however, contends that the origin of negative stereotypes needs to be found in a past that precedes the appearance of whites on Mexico's northern frontier.[22]

Negative Mexican stereotypes were pervasive on the pages of early Anglo-American chroniclers. White stereotypes of Mexicans do not originate at the time of the encounters with the politically, culturally, and economically underdeveloped Mexican northern frontier societies. Dehumanizing depictions were actually applied to Mexicans of the northern frontier and everywhere else.[23] Contempt drove the pens of Anglo-American writers such as Stephen Austin. Austin visited Mexico

City in the period between 1822 and 1823. Austin was convinced of the primitivism of Mexicans, who only lacked tails to distinguish them from apes.[24] Austin was only one of numerous Anglo-American visitors to Mexico City in the nineteenth century who expressed racism toward the people.

Weber contends that close examination of the politics of culture shows how American attitudes toward Mexicans betray anti-Catholic and anti-Spanish viewpoints acquired by Anglo-Americans from their Protestant English culture base. English Protestant culture was not just anti-Catholic; the English also formulated negative images of Spaniards, which historians refer to as the "Black Legend."[25] For instance, Spaniards were viewed as despotic, bigoted, lazy, and cruel. Spanish writers like Bartolome de las Casas, who criticized the brutality of the institution of slavery, were used by the English to serve the purposes of Spanish derision.[26] While the "Black Legend" predisposed Anglos to view Mexicans negatively, white society's abhorrence of racial admixture reinforced negative perceptions.

Mexican racial admixture or *mestizaje* was scorned by Anglo-Americans who believed in the inferiority of mixed blood. Negative Mexican stereotypes legitimated United States' expansionism by presuming the superiority of white culture. The ideology of Manifest Destiny articulated this understanding of the politics of culture. White society's doctrine of Manifest Destiny fueled the United States' expansionist interests not only in the conquest of Mexico, but also in the war with Spain that issued forth in the annexation of Puerto Rico, Guam, and the Philippines in 1898. Racist encounters with Latinos persist today as evidenced in the English-only movement and the consistent negative images of Latinos projected by dominant culture.

Mexicans have experienced downward mobility and heightened racial conflict in white society, whose very institutions negate the distinct cultural otherness of Latinos. Mexicans suffered extreme forms of racial violence in the Southwest, especially between 1900 until the end of the Mexican revolutions in 1925.[27] Systematic lynching of Mexicans by angry whites in the Southwest was common in the nineteenth and early twentieth centuries.[28] Between 1900 and 1965, Mexicans were imported to provide cheap labor for ranch, railway, agricultural, and construction work. Massive deportations have also typified the experience of Mexican immigrants.

Mexicans became highly urbanized following the two world wars and the Great Depression. Ethnic awareness in the context of white society issued forth in a growing political leadership. Barrios in the 1950s saw the development of community organizations that formed the pre-terrain of the Chicano mobilization of the civil rights years. In 1965, the bracero program, a contract labor program agreed upon by the American and Mexican governments to meet labor shortages beginning in the period of World War II, was abolished.[29] Meanwhile, Cesar Chavez invoked cultural and religious symbols to capture the political energies of the Mexican community in labor-organizing efforts.[30] Mexican reality challenges the notion of the "melting pot" with a unique cultural identity that is inseparable from the politics of culture, and that reaches back to the first encounters between Mexicans and an expanding white society in the border states.

The Mexican experience in white society has received a rich theological and Christian ethical articulation over the last thirty years. Indeed, the Mexican-American theologian Virgilio Elizondo expounds a theology of *mestizaje* in his work focused on Jesus' Galilean identity as the starting point for language about God.[31] Galilee was a context of racial admixture that was looked down upon by established Jewish society. However, God's Word for humanity breaks forth into history in the flesh of poverty and rejected humankind. The scandal of God is to choose racial impurity as the point of departure for the kingdom of God at hand. Mexicans and Mexican culture history reveal God to white society with the voice of human agony, struggle, and visionary hope.

**Puerto Ricans**: Puerto Rico was officially incorporated into white society in 1898 following the conclusion of the Spanish-American War. Puerto Ricans have had a different experience of incorporation into American life. The United States has maintained social hegemony in Puerto Rico since 1898 by way of a U.S. military presence, judicial control by the U.S. Congress and executive branch, and economic control by North American business and financial institutions. You may wish to examine the culture history presented in my book *Hear the Cry!* for more details. Below I would like to offer a personal account about my experience of God-talk viewed from the particularity of the barrio.

Puerto Rican settlements were first established in Harlem and Brooklyn at the time of World War I. In the post–World War II period, settlements developed in the South Bronx and Lower Manhattan. Puerto Ricans have not experienced economic prosperity as a result of their ties to the United States; rather, United States rule in Puerto Rico has largely resulted in the steady growth of severe poverty, rapid

# *Remembering*

life escapes me with each breath
and memories burn in the heart in
search of answers: I can see you now

coiling like an axed snake in death's
dance entering the land of silence but
unable to know it would be your last

good-bye. I can hear the long blade
of a knife cutting into Nelson's stomach,
itself starved for food, claiming that life

for a ten-dollar bag of dope. I remember
Simpson Street the whores sold their asses
for petty-cash to johns too poor to pay more

and too strung out to care. I can feel rage
today provoked by the memory of the rape of
the little child Rosa who now feels condemned

to a pain that never leaves. I still smell the
blood that poured down my mother's face the night
she was mugged in the hallway of the building. she

walked up the five flights of stairs to her
apartment, hand pressed against the wound, tearless.
I recall the women raising the children and working

in factories because the men had long lost all
strength to alcohol and sadness. I know the stench
of tenements that imprison Puerto Rican lives like

the Roman cross that crushes the life of innocents
each day in the name of wealth. we wait in those
tenements talking to God in our suffering throwing our

Latino life on the altar of redemption hoping it
will find a way to come through us. . . .

urbanization, social dependency, racial discrimination, enormous drug and alcohol problems, mass migration, and the threat of cultural genocide. Over half of all Puerto Rican families in the states are headed by women. It was Puerto Rican women who raised children in poverty in the South Bronx where I spent my formative years.

Over 50 percent of all Puerto Ricans are born and largely raised in the United States. These second-generation Puerto Ricans, or Nuyoricans, are found all across the nation. The Nuyoricans have produced vital forms of cultural expression in music, theater, dance, and literature that powerfully explain their cultural experience. Nuyorican writers such as Piri Thomas, Marita Morales, Pedro Pietri, Hal Recinos, Miguel Algarin, Nicholasa Mohr, Pedro Juan Soto, Tato Laviera, Miguel Pinero, and José Angel-Figueroa treat such themes as cultural and racial identity, criticism of American culture, distrust of religion, drug problems, and dreams crushed by the injustices of poverty.[32] Nuyorican poets project women as defenders of culture. We mythologize the Puerto Rican mother who symbolizes the defense of Puerto Ricanness.

One of the supreme metaphors in the church's language about God is the family. Typically, the divine family is constructed in terms of a patriarchal and nuclear model. Puerto Rican family fragmentation in the context of the barrio dismantled the patriarchally constructed image of the holy family for me. It was in seminary that I first encountered my antipathy for language about God based on the family metaphor. In a classroom discussion about the character of God's love, the image of the loving "Father" was invoked, causing me to feel theologically alienated. Having grown up in a household without a father, the use of the term "Father" to describe God's love made no sense. For me, God was a mother who expressed love toward her children in a world structured to crush Mother-God and her agonized creation.

**Cubans:** The third largest Latino culture group in the United States is represented by the Cubans. Cuba was also annexed following the signing of the Treaty of Paris in 1898. The Treaty placed Puerto Rico, Guam, and the Philippines in the hands of the United States. However, Cuban independence would come in 1902. Cuban cultural history reflects a different process of incorporation in the structural life of society in North America. Prior to the Cuban Revolution in 1959, Cuban immigrant cigar manufacturers had settled in Key West and Tampa, Florida. However, the Cuban Revolution caused an unprecedented number of Cubans to leave their country and settle mostly in Miami, Florida.[33]

Cuban race and class structure are largely evidenced in the out-migration process that begins with the Cuban Revolution and continues through the arrival of the Marielitos in the 1980s. Marielitos are Cuban refugees who came by way of the Cuban port of Mariel. Ninety percent of the first arrivals were white, professional, educated, and of economic means. Considered refugees from a communist order, these Cubans were subsidized by the federal government. Cuban refugees from this group also resettled in Puerto Rico, moving easily into the upper ranks of society. The second group of Cubans fleeing revolutionary society was over 80 percent white, younger, and poorer. Like the first wave, however, this group was politically conservative. The last wave of Cubans to arrive were the Marielitos in the early 1980s. Forty percent of this group were nonwhite. Many of the 125,000 Cubans of the Mariel boat lift were younger, and the poorest among Cuban refugee groups.[34] Hundreds of Marielitos are still warehoused in prisons across the United States existing as forgotten people.

**Salvadorans**: The most recent Latino arrivals are Central Americans. Unlike the Cubans, Central Americans such as Salvadorans who consider themselves refugees are not recognized in that status by the federal government. El Salvador is the smallest republic in Central America, about the size of Massachusetts, with a population of about five million. El Salvador's political and economic structures were transformed over the last two decades of the nineteenth century through legislated changes in land ownership favoring a coffee-growing oligarchy of fourteen families. Peasant protests against the restructured economy resulted in brutal repression. In 1932, thirty thousand peasants were slaughtered over a one-month period.

More recently, the civil war in El Salvador has produced a death-toll of seventy-five thousand persons and pushed the nation into a foreign debt of over a billion dollars.[35] Because of the eleven-year-old struggle, 25 percent of the people live in refugee status scattered in countries around the world. One million Salvadorans live in the United States—one hundred and fifty thousand in the Washington, D.C. area alone.[36] Salvadorans in the United States experience cultural isolation, fear of deportation, war-related psycho-emotional trauma, poverty and "nonperson" status. Refugees say that to know the meaning of Salvadoran life, it is necessary to understand the meaning of existence experienced between suffering and death.

One Salvadoran I know said of his experience, "The poor suffer, die, have pain, scars . . . people must know. I started to talk. Salvadoran refugees dream of their country, families, and home. Letters from home say death is still there. It is hard to receive these letters . . . My wife is dead. El Salvador is dying, the church is martyred, most people do not know." Ironically, President Duarte feared the possibility of having thousands of Salvadorans in the United States returned following the passage of the Immigration Reform and Control Act (1986). Most Salvadorans were ineligible for amnesty because they arrived after January 1, 1982. In 1987, President Duarte asked Reagan to grant political asylum to Salvadorans, especially because the greatest source of economic aid to El Salvador was refugee export capital. Between 600 million and a billion dollars is sent to El Salvador yearly by the Salvadorans resident in the United States.[37]

God-talk for this community centers on the experience of exile. God walks with a people seemingly abandoned to their exilic suffering in Caesar's household consumed by memories of death.[38] Pastoral anthropology seeks to understand the situation of the Central American "other" in light of cultural history situated in a critical sociopolitical, economic, and biblical-theological analysis. Globalization as the encounter with Salvadoran humanity means discovering the birth of a new church in the justice struggles of oppressed children of God wondering about their abandonment. Pastoral anthropology leads to the discovery of Christ present in the crucified histories of people shattered by the politics of power, but fashioning a culture of protest and resistance.

In 1988, a major popular organization named the National Debate for Peace in El Salvador was founded to broaden the terms of debate for peace. The National Debate is composed of over eighty organizations representing ten subdivisions of society. Membership includes labor, peasant, aboriginal, humanitarian, small- and medium-sized companies, and women's groups. Moreover, religious groups are represented by the Catholic church, base Christian communities, Baptists, Episcopalians, and Lutherans. Civil war has not resulted in established democracy, a strong economy, development, or peace with justice.[39] Thus, the National Debate seeks through its broad representation of Salvadoran society to instill peace with justice through political negotiation. The National Debate has recently opened an office in the nation's capital for lobbying and organizing purposes.[40] On January 16, 1992, a peace accord was signed in Mexico City between the U.S.-backed Salvadoran government and the

Farabundo Martí National Liberation Leadership. The peace accord introduces a new frame of reference for bringing the twelve-year civil war to a conclusion. Solidarity work must now ensure that the terms of peace are implemented. Moreover, the U.S. government must be urged to replace military aid with social and economic development.

Four major Latino cultural groups were briefly and selectively examined to demonstrate the importance of situating the Latino "other" in cultural history. The encounter with the Mexican community in the Southwest reflects a politics of culture with roots in the oppositional history that existed between Protestant English and Spanish Catholic cultural orders. White racism, xenophobia, and feelings of cultural superiority are partly the legacy of the so-called "Black Legend." Puerto Ricans and Mexicans experienced dispossession from the land. Cubans arrived in three waves. The *mariel* wave has received the poorest treatment in American society. Salvadorans have fled their country over the last decade, but have not received refugee status in the United States. Each Latino group has a unique history of contact with white society.

Pastoral anthropology insists on grasping the specific character of cultural experience. For instance, Latino cultural groups manifest a unique set of historical factors that explains concepts of self-identity, faith hermeneutics, and perceptions of white society. Latino religion is a meaning-system partly fashioned against the background of white society's expansionism and political economy. Thus, global encounter with the non-North Atlantic cultural "other" requires white Christianity to listen to the reconstructed God-talk of oppressed humanity. Listening to the oppressed-poor leads to a rereading of the Scriptures as the subversive memory of oppressed humanity. I now turn to the exploration of immersion techniques for ecclesial communities designed to facilitate global encounter in the city.

# CHAPTER SIX

# PASTORAL ANTHROPOLOGY AND LOCAL IMMERSION

P astoral anthropology aims to provide ecclesial communities with a contextual and historical understanding of the dynamics in the human experience of other cultural communities. Encounters with other cultures leads the membership of the local church to new levels of awareness and action serving the interests of justice and humanization in the world. Church experience in a global key directs Christian ethical practice toward the task of transforming social relations in history in light of the good required by God that demands justice for the poor (Micah 6:6-8). I now turn to the exploration of immersion techniques for ecclesial communities designed to facilitate global encounter in the city.

## THE STUDY OF CULTURE:
## IMMERSION IN EVERYDAY LIFE

**Stage I:** The local church will need to form a cultural research group devoted to the task of studying the culture of other social groups. Establishing a *Cultural Domain Listening Group* begins by identifying a group of persons committed to cross-cultural study and enrichment. The Listening Group will be primarily responsible for the study of culture by immersion in the everyday life of specific cultural groups across many social situations. The Listening Group will interpret to the larger ecclesial fellowship the different life-ways of human communities about which little or no knowledge prevails in the local church.[1]

Core membership in the group ought to be limited to six to ten persons. Cross-cultural encounter that leads to local ecclesial and personal transformation characterized by commitment to the practice of justice at the local level, but understood within a global context, is the group's ultimate goal. Following the constitution of the group, a

# *Jamaica in El Bronx*

standing on the corner beside
the big yellow car watching "big
Jamaica Joe" making it shine prior

to the ride down old Grand Concourse
Avenue. you remember kingston as if
it were just yesterday. you lived in

the big house with maids, a cook,
a tyrant aunt, a neighborhood whose
status you never recognized but see

now on television shows that feature
the great american dream you will never
know. Kingston was a place in a house

among a family that wished you'd never
come at all, a sunday outing to church
where even the pet dog it seemed stood

at the altar rail waiting for communion,
the family across the street with a blind
grandfather that the kids walked into trees

for a cruel child's laugh, a father that
never visited there at his sister's house.
now, you come out of the liquor store with

a bottle of wine tucked firmly beneath your
arm yet another ticket to kingston town. looking
around before each "sip" you wonder where

everyone has gone but it does not matter
in the bronx where the buildings keep
falling and you keep taking another swig

only to stop laughing. . . .

decision needs to be made regarding the subject of study. For instance, if the Listening Group decides to study the Latino experience it can begin with a generalized period of intellectual reflection over the course of six weeks. Literature and films can be consulted to establish an "insider's" perspective on the Latino experience as part of the "pre-terrain" for immersion.[2]

**Immersion:** Initial contact with another cultural community requires communication with a mediating person or local institution. The Listening Group can identify such persons and institutions from local community-based newspapers, community organization directories, letter-writing strategies, grass-roots associations such as the church, or direct telephone conversations with known local community leaders. Several group members ought to enter the contact community to observe community dynamics from the perspective of the contact culture. Group members are to have informal conversations with persons in the local context conducted in a variety of settings such as laundromats, restaurants, grocery stores, community meetings, churches, and public gatherings of all types.

Informal conversations with persons from the selected local context will identify themes in people's thinking and culture. At this stage, group members are focused on how the specific contact community views its life and problems. For instance, informal conversations in the nation's capital with Salvadorans put me in touch with that community's cultural thematics. Salvadorans in the nation's capital speak of themselves as a community living between suffering and death. Informal conversation in restaurants, grocery stores, public gatherings, churches, and refugee rights associations unveiled the existential side of the civil war as fear and death, cultural isolation, poverty, psycho-emotional war trauma, and the vision of hope for the creation of a just society.

Group members are to observe the local community's material culture discerning its significant themes. For instance, during walks through the local Salvadoran community, informal conversations were significantly reinforced by observation of material culture. Political posters intended to awaken the public to the reality of the civil war and the plight of Salvadoran refugees in the States, line the streets in the Mount Pleasant and Adams Morgan areas of Washington, D.C. Cultural themes are also communicated in the Salvadoran community on the sides of building walls where murals have been painted portraying community struggles and hope. The beliefs and world view

# American Dream

there are rooms in the South Bronx
cold like the street winter with
walls threatening to crumble beneath

the cries of humanity inside. a new
face is worn by the American dream on the
front steps of our building where the young

children are no longer to be found cause
they fill the cemetery plots on the other
side of town. in madness knives extinguish

life staining memories with the blood of
our brothers and sisters who never knew
the meaning of the dream so much revered

on the soil of America. the neighborhood
remembers the day you, Joseph, met death
in violent convulsions on a dirty rooftop

a needle settled in your vein. now, you
shall see that poor mother of yours who
died of factory-work before her time in

a world that never notices such things.
and life goes on here just the other day
the old women talked of Puerto Rico

to which the mother of the little girl
shot by the stray bullet of a drug pusher's
gun has returned to shed the terror of her
American dream and never

be the same. . . .

of cultural communities are often communicated in such forms of popular cultural discourse.

Spray-painted message systems represent another form of cultural discourse, producing and reflecting cultural thought and behavior. Writing on the sides of many buildings in the Latino section of the nation's capital displays the words, "Oscar Romero Ora Pro Nobis" (Oscar Romero Pray for Us). Much of the political graffiti reveals a pattern of thought indicative of cross-cultural and class solidarity. One slogan reads, "Stop the war in Central America and on the D.C. Poor." Slogans have appeared since the eruption of the Mount Pleasant Riots in May of 1991, articulating the discontent of the Latino community. Cultural discourse of this kind manifests an innate critique of established society that questions systems of structured oppression.

Listening Group members are to read these forms of cultural communication for meaning like a text. Particular attention ought to be given to themes that contest the established order of society, because they represent special moments of insight into the way people and things are classified in a culture. Thus, the initial stage of familiarization with the contact community entails engagement in participant observation and formal and informal conversation with persons from the local context. Members of the Listening Group ought to cultivate a sense of awareness for the details of the social process of the community where the immersion is taking place. Moreover, it is important that the immersion team members develop a good memory of their immersion in local life. Constructing an account of the experience depends on a highly developed capacity to recollect events, conversations, and processes.

## DISCOVERY STRATEGIES

Below are suggestions for conducting the early stages of research in the immersion situation. The series of questions is to be used as a guide by the Listening Group. Remember that these questions are intended to supplement those which the Listening Group has formulated in light of its contextualized experiences and knowledge of the "local talk." Because the Listening Group will establish contacts with local churches in an immersion context, the discovery strategy questions that follow focus on both the local church and community contexts.

In the church setting, note:

• **The physical order of church space.** Where are services held? How is the room arranged? What theological and cultural symbols dominate the church space? Do church members identify with the symbols? How do persons interpret the meaning of church space? Who uses the church during the week besides the congregation? What language system is used to communicate on church bulletin boards (e.g., English, Spanish, Korean, French, and so forth)? How does the leadership and membership of the church describe the purpose of the space? What is it that makes the church sacred? Does the space itself participate in the sacred? Are events the source of sacralization? Do persons' theology of church space carry over into other contexts? What kinds of banners or symbols articulate the space?

• **The church's social structure.** How many people attend church? Who attends: men, women, children, blacks, Asians, Native Americans, Latinos, and so forth? What is the generational composition of the church? What is the leadership structure in terms of gender, age, race, culture, ideology? What is the class structure of the church? What pattern exists between the congregation's demographic picture and that of the surrounding community? How is the congregation's demographic reality related to issues of identity and the social structure of the wider community? Does the church's social structure reflect changes in the local community? What is the family structure? What kinds of family structure exist in the church? Whose culture mediates interpretations of social interaction and reality? Are there any special symbols that reflect or reinforce particular church structures? Who are the poor in the context of the church's social structure?

• **Ritual life and theological identity.** What special objects are part of the congregation's ritual life and local identity? Outside of the ordained clergy, who plays a ritual role in the life of the church—class, race, sex, culture, age? How are rituals such as the Lord's Supper and Baptism interpreted by the local church membership? Are these rituals primarily seen as spiritual events or are they related to everyday concerns? Does the church have a central ritual process constitutive of its sense of identity and community? How do members of the church identify themselves in the Christian tradition (e.g., who is God, Moses, the prophets, Christ, Mary, and so forth)?

What are the theological themes and images communicated in sermons, liturgies, and organizational behavior that influence church identity? Does theology center on private and individual themes or public and corporate ones? How does church ritual relate to local processes of social change? Are there special cultural metaphors used in worship to communicate self-identity? What do these metaphors say about the community? Does theological discourse relate persons to the world, increase human awareness of conflict in social reality or foster retreat from worldly affairs? Is history understood as the context of preparing the way of the Lord? How is politics reflected in the church identity? What political themes are seen in the scriptural record?

In the local community setting, note:

• **The social character of the local context.** What do you observe on walking through the community? How many clearly definable neighborhoods are within walking distance of the immersion team's primary contact base organization? How are these neighborhoods named by the members of local culture? Are the neighborhoods similar or different in terms of racial, ethnic, cultural, linguistic, and socioeconomic composition? What are the boundary markers discernible between neighborhoods? What kinds of social events posters or flyers get posted in public? Do churches have any public image in the community, especially in relation to the poor? What kinds of grass-roots organizations exist in the local community? What do they say about perceived neighborhood problems and concerns? What groups tend to congregate on the street corners and parks? Are there divisions of time throughout the day that change the composition of public gatherings on the neighborhood streets? Do local churches from different class, race and/or cultural traditions have contact with each other?

• **Community social structure.** What links exist between religious and local community organizations? What are the central community issues? What community issues were the focus of neighborhood attention? What local organizations dealt with the central concerns of the neighborhood? What new people are moving into the community? How have organizations such as the church related to newcomers? How does the neighborhood housing, race, ethnic, and class pattern impact the structure of community relationships? Where do various groups interact? How do different cultural groups perceive each other? What are the culturally defined boundaries that promote and/or inhibit social interaction in the local context? How is the community power structure perceived by local members? What group

# *The Corner*

remember the corner where
Tito stood day after another
waiting for something to happen

dispensing advice to the wounded
giving names to the stray dogs roaming
the block in search of food beneath

the shattered bricks and wood of
falling tenements. remember the laundromat
where he would go to wrap himself

away from the cold winter winds and
share a bottle of wine with friends
too stoned to think their names. how

about the time Tito told about
the tears that burned the cheeks
of his face pouring one cold night

while he was buried underneath the
rags he collected from garbage bags
and church rummage sales. Tito stood

days on end on the corner watching
everyone walk away into the horizon
of another block.

or groups hold power in the community? How does that power get institutionalized and distributed? How is power perceived by members of the community? What concepts of community are held by persons in the local context? Are there different ideas of the meaning of community held by different local groups?

• **Community ceremonial life.** What local community ceremonies can be identified by members of the local context? Do public ceremonies at the local level create solidarity? When do ritual events such as street fairs or neighborhood block parties occur in the course of a year? What themes constitute the subject of regularized public ritual events such as street fairs? What public ritual events are deemed of importance for the identity of the local community? What is the structure of religious presence in the local ceremonies? Are sacred symbols in the community religious or nonreligious? How does the church maintain social influence in the local context? How do grass-roots organizations extend their sphere of influence in the community (e.g., street festivals, sponsored community educational forums, and so forth)? What rituals related to the yearly calendar expressive of community solidarity are celebrated in the local context? Who sponsors the public events? Do local community struggles interpenetrate the language and rituals of the contact local church?

## LEARNING ABOUT THE LOCAL CULTURE: KEY INFORMANTS

**Stage II:** After the initial stage of immersion, the Listening Group will have identified several persons with whom to deepen sociocultural analysis in the local context. These persons are referred to in the anthropological literature as key informants. Key informants are persons who are members of the local cultural community. The Listening Group participates in the life of a sociocultural group by observing local events, listening to the way local language classifies reality and conducting face-to-face interviews in the local context with key informants. The Listening Group's initial encounters in the immersion setting will help it formulate questions for the key informant in the local talk.

Generally, anthropologists conduct research with the help of key informants. Persons from the local context are in the best position to provide the Listening Group with detailed and specialized information

# *South Bronx Street*

a stain on the corner that
keeps spreading like oil on paper
doesn't make distinctions when it

appears following blood let from
the human frame that bellows pain
in the air to hang on clouded windows

of tenements. caution has become the
guide for existence on these streets
which claim voices each day thrusting

familiar faces into the silence of
a homicidal abyss. the pentecostal
storefronts tell us Jesus saves for

he knows a thousand deaths in the South
Bronx day after day and no one finds such
words surprising. the crucified lord was

seen on Southern Boulevard just last
week getting stabbed by the Pepsi-Cola
brothers the biggest dope fiends in the

neighborhood under the name of just
another "spik." again, he was found
screaming in the hallway of building

526 on Longfellow Avenue the night
Esther's common law husband came home
laid off from work to beat his wife

and her little puppy friend into the
corridor floor. and the people know
divine mystery on these streets in

the form of wondering why the storefronts
and the churches resign them all to
death on the road to Emmaus that never

finds the stranger. . . .

about the local culture. Key informants are persons that have fervently reflected on the patterns of life and meaning constitutive of the social experience of their local culture. Conversations with key informants may be conducted formally and/or informally. To begin, the Listening Group can informally invite key informants to describe from their point of view a variety of situations in the local context.

On the one hand, the formal interview consists of creating a series of questions or standardized stimuli of any kind such as photos, statistics, and literature to trigger responses in the key informant.[3] The Listening Group could ask the key informant to walk through the local community with a camera photographing scenes thought to define oppression. Photos can later be used to discuss the concept of oppression that was rendered in the perspective of the informer. On the other hand, informal interviews occur all the time in any situation in which persons encounter each other in the flow of daily life. The Listening Group's task here consists of exploring issues and concerns that are raised by the key informant in the process of talk.

The primary objective of the Listening Group consists of understanding the world view, as well as the cultural meaning-system of the contact community. Human behavior is always culturally constituted and saturated with meaning. Thus, the Listening Group needs to concentrate its efforts on more than mere description of observed patterns of social interaction in the local context. The Listening Group has the task of discovering the cultural frame of meaning responsible for the organization of thought and behavior in the immersion community.[4] To this end, discussions with key informants will provide the Listening Group with a culturally constructed interpretation of situations that exist in the local culture.

Below are suggestions for the conduct of interviews. Clearly, the key informant interviewing will proceed along channels identified as significant in the process of the immersion experience. The collection of questions, which focus on the church and community context, are simply designed to help get the Listening Group started. Naturally, the Listening Group has by now collected enough data and samples of "local talk" to be able to phrase questions in terms of language typical of the local context. Remember that informal interviews enable key informants to freely tell the story of their community. Formal interviews are structured around questions developed to get answers to specific concerns.

The Listening Group will ask:

• **In the church setting.** How did you become a member? Why did you become a member? What is your idea of the ideal church community? What would you like to have changed about your church? What one characteristic especially typifies the church? Who have been the pastors and when did they serve? What are the key issues facing the church? How has the church changed over time? What are the church community's ultimate concerns? How does this church view itself in relation to the local community? Who are the church leaders?

• **The ecclesial social structure.** What missions have been organized by the church? What are the community problems? Where do various population segments interact—in the neighborhood, church, social service agencies, and community power structure? Have you actively participated in an issue faced by the local community? Does the church and its religious leaders get involved in public policy issues in the local community? What political and public policy issues are affecting the local community surrounding the church? What would you say is the dominant cultural meaning-system of the church? How are other cultural communities in the local context perceived by church members? What is the language of worship? How many language systems are reflected in the membership? What does linguistic diversity mean for the life of the church?

• **Ritual life and theological identity.** What role does ritual (symbolic dramatizations of ultimate reality) play in encouraging or discouraging local community identity? What are your own religious beliefs? What rituals of the church are important to your own sense of Christian identity? Who is Jesus Christ for the church's identity today? What role does the church's theological identity play in constructing social reality in the local community? Where is God incarnate in the life of the local community? Has the church's theological identity changed over time? How is the church meeting new community needs? How does the church understand itself in relation to other cultural and religious communities? Who are the poor in Jesus' message and for your church? Does the ritual life of the church promote authentic encounter with the cultural "other" or does it maintain boundaries?

## DISCOVERY STRATEGY: MAPPING

The mapping strategy can be implemented now that the Listening Group has increased familiarity with the local setting and local contacts have been made. The mapping strategy enables the Listening Group to locate people in physical space in light of the local knowledge defining cultural boundaries in the neighborhood. First, the Listening Group ought to draw a map of the local community, detailing the relationships that exist between community segments such as settlement patterns and institutional resources. Second, the Listening Group members are to ask local informants to locate themselves in physical space by also drawing a map. Comparison of the two sets of maps will reveal differences in the cultural knowledge defining social reality.

Below are suggestions for the conduct of mapping:
- Begin by mapping the residence and business pattern in the local context. These patterns may reveal the culturally defined boundaries that exist between groups.
- Map a discrete area of the urban environment noting the various kinds of social resources available to community members.
- Following the immersion teams' mapping task, have local people map the significant relationships in the local geography. You will develop a clearer picture about how the community is defined by the local culture.
- Maps published by the local government are useful starting points for this project.

## THE LIFE HISTORY APPROACH TO KEY INFORMANTS

Though conducting a life history requires an extended period of time, it is worth the effort, given the depth and illumination it contributes to field research. Life histories reveal how culture shapes historical perceptions, values, and ideological stances within individual consciousness.[5] The Listening Group will find it useful to conduct a life history with key informants in order to discover the kinds of situations that exist and are faced by the contact community. If the Listening Group has established a level of rapport sufficient to enlist this research strategy with a key informant, it will want to develop a series of questions to guide the interview process. Below are suggestions for conducting a life history interview:[6]
- Begin with open-ended questions: "Tell me about your life as a child." "What was it like to grow up in_____?" "How have you experienced culture change in your life?" "What are the sources of your personal identity?"

- Remember questions raised by previous sessions and ask the informant in the present interview session.
- Work out a sequential event history to provide a framework for the information acquired at each session. You may consider using a time line:

/_____/

birth——childhood experiences——adulthood

Use of the time line illumines the relationship between history and biography.[7]

- Life histories may be event-centered. Thus, you would ask: "Where were you when _____ happened? How have changes in the church and society over _____ years affected your life?"
- Use a tape recorder to facilitate the narrative flow. The recorded material will help the writing process later when you produce the holistic ethnographic account of the local culture. Verbal citations from the life history narrative can be used in ethnographic writing.
- Remember to protect the identity of your informant. I suggest that the immersion team use a code name, unless otherwise instructed by the key informant.

Life history research will enable the immersion team to examine the way society shapes individual identity. Life histories situate human perceptions of the self in history and social process. For instance, in the context of the cultural meaning system of Anglo-American society, persons of Latin American heritage are all categorized "hispanic." This identity marker imposed by society on diverse groups of people of Latin American heritage raises identity questions. One friend of mine came to the states from a country in South America. Jacobo never thought of himself as a "hispanic," rather, his concept of the self was based on a sense of national identity. Jacobo is still dealing with the implications of "hispanic" as a cultural classification system that defines self-image.


## ENCOUNTER AS TRANSFORMATION

**Stage III:** The information gathered by the Listening Group is now ready to be presented to the larger church audience. Persons in the church who have not had any contact with the subject community will require the cultural meaning system of the immersion community to be clearly communicated. The Listening Group will need to adequately represent the cultural patterns, values, beliefs, and behavior of the contact community. Special attention should be given to the specific character of common life as it was experienced by the immersion team. Focusing on the distinctive aspects of observed daily existence helps persons not familiar with another cultural community to develop a feeling for the people described.

The Listening Group will need to unfold an analysis of the data collected in the field. Preferably, data analysis ought to be driven by the categories related by informants in the field. For instance, during periods of fieldwork with the Salvadoran refugee community, I discovered that life histories fall into two categories. First, life histories can be categorized under the heading of *suffering and death*. Salvadoran refugees in the United States relate that life for them is an experience between suffering and death. Life histories disclose that many Salvadoran refugees are suffering from Post Traumatic Stress Disorder (PTSD). PTSD is typified by feelings of extreme depression, anxiety, and flashbacks to horrifying war experiences in El Salvador. Salvadoran refugees live under conditions of marginality in the United States that take the form of extreme poverty and isolation.

Second, the next informant heading is that of *empowerment and life*. Salvadoran refugees relate how they draw strength from the history of Christian social martyrs who have taught them the value of laying down one's life for a friend. The supreme martyr symbol of empowerment and life for Salvadoran refugees is Archbishop Oscar Romero. More recently, the six Jesuits and their two employees killed in November of 1989 have been incorporated into life history narratives of empowerment and life. Salvadoran refugees feel empowered to struggle for life as they exercise sacred remembrance on the anniversaries of the death of Oscar Romero (March 24) and the six Jesuits and their two employees (November 16). Hence, time has the quality of Kairos, fueling the sentiment of empowerment and life manifested in the struggle for justice.

Plainly, local church communities need to place social reality at the center of their theological reflection. Language about the plight of Salvadoran refugees in the United States can never substitute for the evangelizing potential of direct encounter with the Salvadoran refugee community. Thus, transformation in the parish will not come from merely talking about God's concern for justice in human community;

instead, any theology of justice must make concrete reference to the struggle of specific sociocultural groups engaged in the process of overcoming conditions of injustice and oppression.

## CONCLUSION

Pastoral anthropology seeks to enable local church communities to enter into an authentic examination of the cultural other. The field method approach outlined above can be adapted to meet the needs of most situations. Human experience is represented by cultural actors in countless ways. The pursuit of local immersion in the life of "other" cultural communities about which little or nothing is known raises church members' awareness regarding how cultural values and symbols organize human experience across society in response to lived historical conditions. Pastoral anthropology is a method for examining cultural meaning as it exists in the symbols and social action of specific communities.

The profound transformation of the church in Latin America resulted from a genuine immersion in the life of the poor and oppressed. The Latin American church opened itself to the Spirit of God moving in the cries of the poor, as they confronted and protested their wretched conditions of life. Latin American Christian anthropology radically historicized the meaning of faith and human subjectivity. Consequently, Jesus Christ is the word become flesh in the poor. History is not only the context of God's revelation expressed in sociopolitical acts of liberation on behalf of the oppressed; but, human beings are also empowered to make history by a God who defends the oppressed by becoming one of them. Church renewal in the United States will depend upon a commitment to rediscover humanity as an agent of history. Immersion approaches to social relations awaken the local church's own sense of agency in history by affirming values based on solidarity, commitment, service, and community.

Forming Listening Groups is the first step toward local immersion. The approach outlined above presumes that local churches need to decide on a contact community in light of their own internal processes and concerns about the relation of faith to society; yet, the biblical record suggests a starting place. Salvation history takes as its point of departure the real history of oppressed Hebrew slaves in Egypt. In Jesus, the ultimate historicization of salvation occurs as God takes on the flesh of poverty in order to reveal humanity's ethical vocation as transformer of history. Thus, immersion begins by initiating an encounter with the poor and oppressed who have been excluded from society's economic and political structures. Local churches discover the meaning of globalization once they are submerged in the historical reality of the marginated in their own context, as well as overseas.

Throughout this book I have argued that the city represents a necessary context for globalization. The techniques outlined in this chapter are designed to help local church communities begin to seek the immersion of the city. Of course, there are churches already involved in broadening their understanding of the faith tradition by dialogue and encounter with other cultural, racial, social, and economic groups; however, these churches remain largely an exception within particular denominational structures. Immersion motivated by a genuine interest in gaining a new faith compass for directing Christian ethical concerns implies steering a course directly to the heart of the city's Latino barrios, black ghettos, and marginal places. Globalization means confronting social reality from a vision of humanity built upon the foundation of the gospel. Faith must be nothing less than a social force in the city seeking to transform social institutions in light of Jesus Christ's promise to oppose dehumanization and oppression.

# NOTES

## CHAPTER 1

1. The term used in the context of the barrio for a street preacher is *evangelica*.

2. Harold J. Recinos, *Hear the Cry!* (Louisville: Westminster/John Knox Press, 1989), chap. 1.

3. On Rudy and the Church of All Nations, see Recinos, *Hear the Cry!*

## CHAPTER 2

1. See Samuel Wilson, "The Field Is the World and the World Is Increasingly Urban," in *Signs of the Kingdom in the Secular City*, ed. David J. Frenchak and Clinton E. Stockwell (Chicago: Covenant Press, 1984).

2. William Dever, "Syro-Palestinian and Biblical Archaeology," in *The Hebrew Bible and Its Modern Interpreters*, ed. Douglas A. Knight and Gene M. Tucker (Philadelphia: Fortress Press, 1985), pp. 31-74.

3. See Ray Bakke, *The Urban Christian* (Downers Grove: Intervarsity Press, 1987); see also David S. Lim, "The City in the Bible," *Evangelical Review of Theology* 12 (1): 138-56.

4. Robert R. Wilson, "The City in the Old Testament," in *Civitas: Religious Interpretations of the City*, ed. Peter S. Hawkins (Atlanta: Scholars Press, 1966), pp. 3-13; Frank S. Frick, *The City in Ancient Israel* (Missoula, Mont.: Scholars Press, 1977), chap. IV.

5. Wilson, "The City in the Old Testament," p. 7.

6. Lim, "The City in the Bible," p. 141.

7. Richard Shaull, *Heralds of a New Reformation* (Maryknoll, N.Y.: Orbis Press, 1985), chap. 1; see also Norman Gottwald, *The Tribes of Yahweh: A Sociology of Israel, 1250-1050 B.C.E.* (Maryknoll, N.Y.: Orbis Press, 1979).

8. Wilson, "City in the Old Testament," p. 9.

9. Walter Brueggemann, *The Prophetic Imagination* (Philadelphia: Fortress Press, 1983), chap. 2.

10. Frick, *The City in Ancient Israel*, p. 230.
11. Ibid.
12. Ibid., pp. 227-31.
13. Wilson, "City in the Old Testament," pp. 10-13.
14. Virgilio Elizondo, *Galilean Journey* (Maryknoll, N.Y.: Orbis Press, 1985), p. 51.
15. Ibid.
16. Recinos, *Hear the Cry!* pp. 71-72.
17. Elizondo, *Galilean Journey*, p. 73.
18. William Lane, *Hebrews: A Call to Commitment* (Peabody, Mass.: Hendrickson Publishers, 1985), chap. I.
19. Wayne A. Meeks, "Saint Paul and the Cities," in *Civitas: Religious Interpretations of the City*, ed. Peter S. Hawkins (Atlanta: Scholars Press, 1986), pp. 17-23.
20. Jack Nelson-Pallmeyer, *The Politics of Compassion* (Maryknoll, N.Y.: Orbis Press, 1988), pp. 9-15; Gustavo Gutiérrez, *The Power of the Poor in History* (Maryknoll, N.Y.: Orbis Press, 1984), pp. 44-46.
21. Nelson-Pallmeyer, *The Politics of Compassion*, p. 13.
22. Ibid., p. 11.
23. Ibid., p. 15.

**CHAPTER 3**

1. See Harvey Cox, *Religion in the Secular City* (New York: Simon & Schuster, 1984).
2. Orlando Costas, *Christ Outside the Gate* (Maryknoll, N.Y.: Orbis Press, 1984), p. 164.
3. Rafael Valdivieso and Cary Davis, "U.S. Hispanics: Challenging Issues for the 1990s," *Population Trends and Public Policy*, 17 (December 1988): 2.
4. Rodolfo O. de la Garza, ed., *The Mexican American Experience* (Austin: University of Texas, 1985), chap. 1.
5. See Rodolfo Acuna, *Occupied America: A History of Chicanos* (New York: Harper & Row, 1981). See also Vine Deloria, *Custer Died for Your Sins* (New York: Avalon, 1969); Cornel West, *Prophecy and Deliverance: An Afro-American Revolutionary Christianity*; Eugene D. Genovese, *From Rebellion to Revolution: Afro-American Slave Revolts in the Making of the New World* (New York: Random House, 1981).
6. See Renny Golden and Michael McConnell, *Sanctuary: The New Underground Railroad* (Maryknoll, N.Y.: Orbis Press, 1986).
7. See Kent Flannery, ed., *The Early Mesoamerican Village* (New York: Academic Press, 1976).
8. See M. L. Fowler, et al., *Perspectives in Cahokia Archaeology* (Illinois Archaeological Survey, Urbana: University of Illinois Press, 1975).
9. Howard P. Chudacoff and Judith E. Smith, *The Evolution of American Urban Society* (Englewood Cliffs, N.J.: Prentice-Hall, 1988), chap. I.; Darcy Ribeiro, *The Civilizational Process*, trans. Betty J. Meggers (New York: Harper & Row, 1968), chap. III.
10. See Vine Deloria and Clifford Lytle, *The Nations Within* (New York: Pantheon Books, 1984).
11. Chudacoff and Smith, *The Evolution of American Urban Society*, see chap. 1.
12. S. Dale McLemore and Ricardo Romo, "The Origins and Development of the Mexican People," in de la Garza, *The Mexican American Experience*, p. 6.
13. Rodolfo Acuna, *Occupied America: A History of Chicanos*, 3rd ed. (New York: Harper & Row, 1987), p. 7.
14. Edna Acosta-Belen, "From Settlers to Newcomers: The Hispanic Legacy in the

United States," in The Hispanic Experience in the United States: Contemporary Issues and Perspectives, ed. Edna Acosta-Belen and Barbara R. Sjostrom (New York: Praeger Books, 1988), pp. 86-87.

15. McLemore and Romo, "The Origins and Development of the Mexican People," pp. 6-7.

16. Acuna, *Occupied America*, chap. 1.

17. Ibid.

18. Frederick A. Norwood, *The Story of American Methodism* (Nashville: Abingdon Press, 1974), p. 265.

19. Chudacoff and Smith, *The Evolution of American Urban Society*, p. 4.

20. Ibid., pp. 8-16.

21. Leonard Dinnerstein and David M. Reimers, *Ethnic Americans: A History of Immigration and Assimilation* (New York: Dodd, Mead and Company), chap. I.

22. See especially Genovese, *From Rebellion to Revolution*.

23. I am especially indebted to Chudacoff and Smith, *The Evolution of American Urban Society*, pp. 16-19; see also Gary B. Nash, *The Urban Crucible: Social Change, Political Consciousness and the Origins of the American Revolution* (Cambridge: Harvard University Press, 1979).

24. Chudacoff and Smith, *The Evolution of American Urban Society*, p. 16.

25. Ibid., p. 17.

26. Ibid., p. 18.

27. Ibid.

28. Ibid., pp. 54-55.

29. Ibid., p. 24.

30. See Nash, *The Urban Crucible*. See also Chudacoff and Smith, *The Evolution of American Urban Society*, pp. 26-35.

31. Acosta-Belen, "From Settlers to Newcomers," p. 88.

32. *El Tiempo Latino*, October 25, 1991.

33. Chudacoff and Smith, *The Evolution of American Urban Society*, pp. 40-41.

34. Ibid., p. 40.

35. Robert T. Handy, *A History of the Churches in the United States and Canada* (Oxford: Oxford University Press, 1976), p. 146.

36. Dinnerstein and Reimers, *Ethnic Americans*, pp. 38-39.

37. Andrew Lees, *Cities Perceived: Urban Society in European and American Thought, 1820-1940* (New York: Columbia University Press, 1985), pp. 92-93.

38. Ibid., pp. 96-97.

39. Ibid., pp. 91-97.

40. See Chudacoff and Smith, *The Evolution of American Urban Society*, pp. 111-17.

41. Dinnerstein and Reimers, *Ethnic Americans*, pp. 57 and 79.

42. Dennis R. Judd, *The Politics of American Cities: Private Power and Public Policy*, 3rd ed. (St. Louis: Harper Collins Publishers, 1988), p. 23.

43. Patrick J. Ashton, "Urbanization and the Dynamics of Suburban Development Under Capitalism," in *Marxism and the Metropolis: New Perspectives in Urban Political Economy*, 2nd ed., ed. William K. Tabb and Larry Sawers (New York: Oxford University Press, 1984), pp. 54-81.

44. Chudacoff and Smith, *The Evolution of American Urban Society*, chaps. 3 and 4; Gary Gappert and Richard V. Knight, "Cities in the 21st Century," *Urban Affairs Annual Review* 23 (1982): 2.

45. See Raymond Carr, *Puerto Rico: A Colonial Experiment* (New York: New York University Press, 1984).

46. Edward H. Spicer, "Urban Indians," in *Harvard Encyclopedia of American Ethnic Groups*, ed. Stephan Thernstrom (Cambridge: Harvard University Press, 1980), pp. 109-14.

47. Jon C. Teaford, *The Twentieth-Century American City* (Baltimore: Johns Hopkins, 1986), p. 57.

48. Acuna, *Occupied America*, pp. 171-72.

49. Ibid., pp. 289-90.

50. Teaford, *The Twentieth-Century American City*, pp. 82-90.

51. Ibid., pp. 84-90.

52. Chudacoff and Smith, *The Evolution of American Urban Society*, pp. 246-47.

53. Teaford, *The Twentieth-Century American City*, pp. 98-109.

54. Chudacoff and Smith, *The Evolution of American Urban Society*, p. 267.

55. Aldon D. Morris, *The Origins of the Civil Rights Movement: Black Communities Organizing for Change* (New York: Free Press, 1984), pp. 50-52.

56. Chudacoff and Smith, *The Evolution of American Urban Society*, p. 278.

57. Ibid., p. 280.

58. Judd, *The Politics of American Cities*, p. 325; Chudacoff and Smith, *The Evolution of American Urban Society*, pp. 284-85; Charles Murray, *Losing Ground: American Social Policy 1950-1980* (New York: Basic Books, 1984).

59. See especially Richard Child Hill, "Fiscal Crisis, Austerity Politics, and Alternative Urban Policies," in Tabb and Sawers, *Marxism and the Metropolis*.

60. Chudacoff and Smith, *The Evolution of American Urban Society*, p. 301.

61. Teaford, *The Twentieth-Century American City*, p. 142.

62. Ibid., p. 143.

63. Ibid., pp. 147-50; see also Chudacoff and Smith, *The Evolution of American Urban Society*, p. 303.

64. Ibid.

65. Judd, *The Politics of American Cities*, p. 7.

66. Recinos, *Hear the Cry!* pp. 60-61.

67. Judd, *The Politics of American Cities*, p. 357.

68. The Korean population in the states grew following the removal of restrictive immigration policies for Asians entering the United States. By 1985, Koreans owned some nine thousand small businesses in New York. Koreans who came to the states were mostly from the upper and middle classes, Protestant, and educated. The small business is the economic base of Korean families in the states. See especially Ilsoo Kim, "The Koreans: Small Business in an Urban Frontier," in *New Immigrants in New York*, ed. Nancy Foner (New York: Columbia University Press, 1987), pp. 219-42.

69. See *A Status Report on Hunger and Homelessness in America's Cities: 1988* (Washington, D.C.: The United States Conference of Mayors, 1989).

70. Ibid.

71. T. Berry Brazelton, "Why Is America Failing Its Children?" *The New York Times Magazine*, 9 Sept. 1990, 42.

72. See *Newsweek*, Winter/Spring 1990.

## CHAPTER 4

1. See Marc H. Ellis, "Notes Toward a Jewish Theology of Liberation," in *Churches in Struggle: Liberation Theology and Social Change in North America*, ed. William Tabb (New York: Monthly Review Press, 1986).

2. James Cone, "Black Theology: Its Origin, Method, and Relation to Third World Theologies," in Tabb, *Churches in Struggle*, pp. 32-33.

3. James Cone, *For My People: Black Theology and the Black Church* (Maryknoll, N.Y.: Orbis Press, 1984), chap. II.

4. Peter Paris, *The Social Teachings of the Black Churches* (Philadelphia: Fortress Press, 1985), p. 4.

5. See Cain Felder, *Troubling Biblical Waters: Race, Class, and Family* (Maryknoll, N.Y.: Orbis Books, 1989); Orlando Costas, "Contextualization and Incarnation: Communicating Christ Amid the Oppressed," in Costas, *Christ Outside the Gate*, pp. 3-20; and Jon Sobrino, "The Promotion of Justice as an Essential Requirement of the Gospel Message," in *The True Church and the Poor* (Maryknoll, N.Y.: Orbis Books, 1984), pp. 39-63.

6. Paris, *The Social Teachings of the Black Churches*, pp. 8-9.

7. Ibid.

8. See especially Cone, *For My People*, chaps. VII, VIII and X.

9. Ibid., chap. X.

10. See Recinos, *Hear the Cry!*

11. See the work of the German theologian Elizabeth Schüssler Fiorenza.

12. See Rosemary Radford Ruether, *Sexism and God-Talk* (Boston: Beacon Press, 1983); see also Virginia Fabella and Mercy Oduyoye, eds., *With Passion and Compassion* (Maryknoll, N.Y.: Orbis Press, 1988).

13. See Micaela di Leonardo, *The Varieties of Ethnic Experience* (Ithaca: Cornell University Press, 1984); Faye Ginsburg "Procreation Stories: Reproduction, Nurturance and Procreation in Life Narratives of Abortion Activists," in *American Ethnologist* (1987): 623-36; and Michelle Z. Rosaldo and Louise Lamphere, *Women, Culture and Society* (Stanford: Stanford University Press, 1974).

14. Gertrude S. Goldberg and Eleanor Kremen, "The Feminization of Poverty: Only in America?" *Social Policy* (Spring 1987): 3.

15. Emily Northrop, "The Feminization of Poverty: The Demographic Factor and the Composition of Economic Growth," *Journal of Economic Issues* (March 1990): 145.

16. Goldberg and Kremen, "The Feminization of Poverty," 3-13.

17. Ibid.

18. See Delores S. Williams, "Womanist Theology: Black Women's Voices," *Christianity and Crisis* (March 2, 1987): 66-70; see also Ada Maria Isasi-Diaz, "Mujeristas: A Name of Our Own" in *The Future of Liberation Theology*, ed. Marc Ellis and Otto Maduro (Maryknoll, N.Y.: Orbis Press, 1989).

19. Tereza Cavalcanti, "The Prophetic Ministry of Women in the Hebrew Bible," in *Through Her Eyes: Women Theology from Latin America*, ed. Elsa Tamez (Maryknoll, N.Y.: Orbis Books, 1989), pp. 121-22.

20. Felder, *Troubling Biblical Waters*, chap. 8.

21. Ibid., pp. 145-48.

22. See especially Lawrence E. Sullivan, ed., *Native American Religions: North America* (New York: Macmillan, 1989).

23. Ibid., chap. II.

24. See George E. Tinker, "The Integrity of Creation: Restoring Trinitarian Balance," *The Ecumenical Review* (October 1989).

25. Dee Brown, *Bury My Heart at Wounded Knee: An Indian History of the American West* (New York: Bantam Books, 1970), p. 1; see also Luis N. Rivera Pagan, *Evangelizacion y Violencia: La Conquista de America* (San Juan, Puerto Rico: Editorial Cemi, 1990), cap. I; and Leonardo Boff, "Exigencias Teologicas e Eclesiologicas para uma Nova Evangelizacao," *Revista Eclesiastica Brasileira* 47 (185): 120-44.

26. Gordon R. Willey and Jeremy A. Sabloff, *A History of American Archaeology* (New York: W. H. Freeman and Company, 1980), chap. III.

27. See James L. West, "Indian Spirituality: Another Vision," *American Baptist Quarterly* (December, 1986).

28. See Louis J. Luzbetak, *The Church and Cultures* (Maryknoll, N.Y.: Orbis Press, 1988); and Robert J. Schreiter, *Constructing Local Theologies* (Maryknoll, N.Y.: Orbis Press, 1986).

29. West, "Indian Spirituality," pp. 354-55.

30. Ibid., p. 350.

31. See William E. Baldridge, "Toward a Native American Theology," *American Baptist Quarterly* (December, 1989).

32. Tinker, "The Integrity of Creation," p. 527.

33. See Baldridge, "Toward a Native American Theology."

34. Jim Rice, "In the Shadow of War," *Sojourners*, April 1991, 5.

35. Jim Wallis, "A Neither Just Nor Holy War," *Sojourners*, April 1991, 11.

36. See *Sojourners*, April 1991; see also Rosemary Radford Ruether, "Religion and War in the Middle East," *Sojourners*, June 1991.

37. Ibid., p. 4.

38. Alixa Naff, "Arabs in America" in *Arabs in the New World: Studies on Arab-American Communities*, ed. Sameer Y. Abraham and Nabeel Abraham (Detroit: Wayne State University, 1983), p. 12.

39. Ibid., p. 13. See also Najib E. Saliba, "Emigration from Syria," in *Arabs in the New World*, p. 32.

40. See Philip M. Kayal, "Arab Christians in the United States," in *Arabs in the New World*.

41. Ibid., p. 46.

42. Ibid., pp. 46-47.

43. Stephen Bevans, "Models of Contextual Theology," *Missiology* 13 (1985): 185.

44. See Costas, *Christ Outside the Gate*; see also Luzbetak, *The Church and Cultures*.

## CHAPTER 5

1. See especially Mark Kline Taylor, "What Has Anthropology to Do with Theology?" *Theology Today* 41 (4): 379-82.

2. See especially Bronislaw Malinowski, *Argonauts of the Western Pacific* (Prospect Heights, Ill.: Waveland Press, Inc, 1987). See also George E. Marcus and Michael M. J. Fisher, *Anthropology as Cultural Critique: An Experimental Moment in the Human Sciences* (Chicago: University of Chicago Press, 1986).

3. See Marcus and Fisher, *Anthropology as Cultural Critique*. See also di Leonardo, *The Varieties of Ethnic Experience*; and June Nash, *We Eat the Mines and the Mines Eat Us: Dependency and Exploitation in Bolivian Tin Mines* (New York: Columbia University Press, 1979).

4. Ginsburg, "Procreation Stories," 623-36. See also Margaret Mead, *Coming of Age in Samoa* (New York: William Morrow and Co., 1973); and Rosaldo and Lamphere, *Women, Culture, and Society*.

5. Pagan, *Evangelizacion y Violencia*, cap. I; Boff, "Exigencias Teologicas e Eclesiologicas para uma Nova Evangelizacao," 120-44.

6. Clifford Geertz, *The Interpretation of Cultures* (New York: Basic Books, 1973), chap. 2.

7. See especially James Lett, *The Human Enterprise: A Critical Introduction to Anthropological Inquiry* (Boulder and London: Westview Press, 1987).

8. Sydney Mintz, *Sweetness and Power: The Place of Sugar in Modern History* (New York: Penguin Books, 1985); William Roseberry, *Anthropologies and Histories: Essays in*

*Culture, History, and Political Economy* (New Brunswick: Rutgers University Press, 1989); and Eric Wolf, *Europe and the People Without History* (Berkeley: University of California Press, 1982).

9. For this school of anthropology, see especially Roseberry, *Anthropologies and Histories;* Gerald M. Sider, *Culture and Class in Anthropology and History: A Newfoundland Illustration* (Cambridge: Cambridge University Press, 1986); Mintz, *Sweetness and Power;* Michael Taussig, *The Devil and Commodity Fetishism in South America* (Chapel Hill: University of North Carolina Press, 1980). See also the pioneer of the school: Wolf, *Europe and the People Without History* (Berkeley: University of California Press, 1982).

10. Valdivieso and Davis, "U.S. Hispanics: Challenging Issues for the 1990s," 5.

11. J. Jorge Klor de Alva, "Telling Hispanics Apart: Latino Sociocultural Diversity," in Acosta-Belen and Sjostrom, *The Hispanic Experience in the United States,* p. 107.

12. See Joan Moore and Harry Pachon, *Hispanics in the United States* (Englewood Cliffs, N.J.: Prentice-Hall, 1985).

13. David Weber, "From Hell Itself: The Americanization of Mexico's Northern Frontier," in *Myth and History of the Hispanic Southwest* (Albuquerque: University of New Mexico Press, 1988), p. 112; see also Acuna, *Occupied America,* chap. 1.

14. Weber, "From Hell Itself," pp. 114-15.

15. Acuna, *Occupied America,* p. 6.

16. Ibid., p. 6.

17. Ibid., pp. 6-7.

18. Ibid., p. 7.

19. Moore and Pachon, *Hispanics in the United States,* p. 19.

20. This section draws on David Weber's "Scarce More than Apes: Historical Roots of Anglo-American Stereotypes of Mexicans in the Border Region," in *Myth and the History of the Hispanic Southwest* (Albuquerque: University of New Mexico Press, 1988), pp. 153-67.

21. Ibid., p. 156.

22. Ibid., p. 156-57.

23. Ibid., pp. 156-59.

24. As quoted in ibid., p. 157.

25. Ibid., p. 159.

26. Ibid., pp. 159-60. See also David Hurst Thomas, "Saints and Soldiers at Santa Catalina: Hispanic Designs for Colonial America," in *The Recovery of Meaning,* ed. M. P. Leone and P. B. Potter (Washington, D.C.: Smithsonian Institution Press, 1988), pp. 73-140.

27. Moore and Pachon, *Hispanics in the United States,* p. 20.

28. See especially Acuna, *Occupied America.*

29. The Second World War created labor shortages in various subdivisions of the North American economy. Women filled part of the labor need during this period, but the lowest-paying jobs remained vacant. Braceros (manual laborers) filled low-paying jobs in agriculture, maintenance, construction, and the railroad divisions of the economy. The wartime contract labor program continued beyond the end of the war, even resulting in the formalization of the agreement between the Mexican and American governments with the passage of Public Law 78 in 1951. All told, the bracero period extended from 1942 until 1964.

30. Moore and Pachon, *Hispanics in the United States,* p. 30.

31. See especially Elizondo, *Galilean Journey.*

32. Joseph P. Fitzpatrick, *Puerto Rican Americans: The Meaning of Migration to the Mainland* (Englewood Cliffs, N.J.: Prentice-Hall, 1987), pp. 179-90.

33. Moore and Pachon, *Hispanics in the United States*, p. 36.

34. Ibid., pp. 35-37.

35. See Elizabeth G. Ferris, *The Central American Refugees* (New York: Praeger Books, 1987).

36. Segundo Montes Mozo and Juan José Garcias Vasquez, *Salvadoran Migration to the United States: An Exploratory Study* (Washington, D.C.: Center for Immigration Policy and Refugee Assistance, Georgetown University, 1988), p. 6.

37. See Ann Crittenden, *Sanctuary: A Story of American Conscience and the Law in Collision* (New York: Weidenfeld and Nicolson, 1988). See also Montes and Vasquez, *Salvadoran Migration to the United States*.

38. See Cristian de la Rosa et al, *Fe y Exilio: The Central American Exile* (Washington, D.C.: Casa del Pueblo, 1459 Columbia Road, N.W., 1990). See also Daniel L. Smith, *The Religion of the Landless: The Social Context of the Babylonian Exile* (Bloomington: Meyer-Stone Books, 1989); and Justo González, *Mañana: Christian Theology from a Hispanic Perspective* (Nashville: Abingdon Press, 1990).

39. Testimony of Reverend Edgar Palacios, "House Subcommittees on Western Hemisphere Affairs and Human Rights and International Organizations," February 6, 1990.

40. For information on the National Debate for Peace, contact Reverend Amparo Palacios at (202) 546-3140, or write: National Debate for Peace in El Salvador, P.O. Box 76385, Washington, D.C. 20013.

## CHAPTER 6

1. Michael H. Agar, *The Professional Stranger: An Informal Introduction to Ethnography* (Orlando: Academic Press, 1980), chap. II.

2. An important preparatory source is Albert Camarillo, *Latinos in the United States: A Historical Bibliography* (Santa Barbara: ABC-CLIO, 1986). See also Leonard Dinnerstein, Roger L. Nichols, and David M. Reimers, *Natives and Strangers: Black, Indians, and Immigrants in America,* 2nd ed. (New York: Oxford University Press, 1990).

3. H. Russell Bernard, *Research Methods in Cultural Anthropology* (Beverly Hills, Calif.: Sage Publications, 1988), chap. 10.

4. James P. Spradley, *Participant Observation* (New York: Holt, Rinehart & Winston, 1980), chap. 5.

5. Nash, *We Eat the Mines and the Mines Eat Us.* See also Agar, *The Professional Stranger,* pp. 105-6.

6. Julia G. Crane and Michael V. Agrosino, *Field Projects in Anthropology: A Student Handbook* (Morristown, N.J.: General Learning Press, 1974), pp. 74-84.

7. Ibid.

# SUGGESTED FURTHER READING

## I. ETHNOGRAPHIC RESEARCH AND ANTHROPOLOGICAL THEORY

Applebaum, Herbert, ed. *Perspectives in Cultural Anthropology.* Albany: State University of New York Press, 1987.

Bee, Robert L. *Patterns and Processes: An Introduction to Anthropological Strategies for the Study of Culture.* New York: Free Press, 1974.

Bernard, Russell H. *Research Methods in Cultural Anthropology.* Newbury, Calif.: Sage Publications, 1988.

Crane, Julia, and Michael V. Agrosino. *Collecting Life Histories: Field Projects in Anthropology.* Prospect Heights: Waveland Press, 1984.

Geertz, Clifford. *The Interpretation of Cultures.* New York: Basic Books, 1973.

Glick, Ronald, and Joan Moore, eds. *Drugs in the Hispanic Communities.* New Brunswick, N.J.: Rutgers University Press, 1990.

Kertzer, David I. *Ritual, Politics and Power.* New Haven: Yale University Press, 1988.

Lehmann, Arthur C., and James E. Meyers, eds. *Magic, Witchcraft, and Religion: An Anthropological Study of the Supernatural,* 2nd ed. Chico: Mayfield Publishing Company, 1989.

Lett, James. *The Human Enterprise: A Critical Introduction to Anthropological Theory.* Boulder and London: Westview Press, 1987.

Moore, Joan, and Harry Pachon. *Hispanics in the United States.* Englewood Cliffs, N.J.: Prentice-Hall, 1985.

Roseberry, William. *Anthropologies and Histories: Essays in Culture, History, and Political Economy.* New Brunswick, N.J.: Rutgers University Press, 1989.

141

Spradley, J. P. *Participant Observation*. New York: Holt, Rinehart & Winston, 1980.

Van Maanen, John. *Tales of the Field: On Writing Ethnography*. Chicago: University of Chicago Press, 1988.

Williams, Brett, ed. *The Politics of Culture*. Washington and London: Smithsonian Institution Press, 1991.

## II. THEOLOGICAL WORKS

Boff, Clodovis, and George V. Pixley. *The Bible, the Church and the Poor*. Maryknoll, N.Y.: Orbis Books, 1989.

Comblin, José. *Retrieving the Human: A Christian Anthropology*. Maryknoll, N.Y.: Orbis Books, 1990.

Cook, Guillermo. *The Expectation of the Poor: Latin American Ecclesial Communities in Protestant Perspective*. Maryknoll, N.Y.: Orbis Books, 1985.

Costas, Orlando. *Christ Outside the Gate*. Maryknoll, N.Y.: Orbis Books, 1982.

Elizondo, Virgilio. *Galilean Journey: The Mexican-American Promise*. Maryknoll, N.Y.: Orbis Books, 1983.

Kirkpatrick, Dow, ed. *Faith Born of the Struggle for Life*. Grand Rapids: Wm. B. Eerdmans, 1988.

Luzbetak, Louis J. *The Church and Cultures: New Perspectives in Missiological Anthropology*. Maryknoll, N.Y.: Orbis Books, 1988.

McGovern, Arthur F. *Liberation Theology and Its Critics: Toward an Assessment*. Maryknoll, N.Y.: Orbis Books, 1989.

Maduro, Otto. *Religion and Social Conflict*. Maryknoll, N.Y.: Orbis Books, 1982.

Schreiter, Robert J. *Constructing Local Theologies*. Maryknoll, N.Y.: Orbis Books, 1986.

Tonna, Benjamin. *Gospel for the Cities*. Maryknoll, N.Y.: Orbis Books, 1985.

## III. WORSHIP MATERIALS

Duck, Ruth C., ed. *Bread for the Journey*. New York: Pilgrim Press, 1981.

Duck, Ruth C., and Maren C. Tirabassi, eds. *Touch Holiness*. New York: Pilgrim Press, 1990.

Esquivel, Julia. *Threatened with Resurrection: Prayers and Poems from an Exiled Guatemalan*. Elgin, Ill.: The Brethren Press, 1982.

Sobrino, Jon. *Spirituality of Liberation: Toward Political Holiness*. Maryknoll, N.Y.: Orbis Books, 1988.

Sobrino, Jon, and Ignacio Martin-Baro, eds. *Archbishop Oscar Romero: Voice of the Voiceless*. Maryknoll, N.Y.: Orbis Books, 1990.

Soelle, Dorothee. *Revolutionary Patience*. Maryknoll, N.Y.: Orbis Books, 1969.